What Does It Mean to Be Well Educated?

Also by Alfie Kohn

No Contest: The Case Against Competition

The Brighter Side of Human Nature: Altruism and Empathy in Everyday Life

You Know What They Say . . . : The Truth About Popular Beliefs

Punished by Rewards: The Trouble with Gold Stars, Incentive Plans, A's, Praise, and Other Bribes

Beyond Discipline: From Compliance to Community

Education, Inc.: Turning Learning into a Business [editor]

What to Look for in a Classroom . . . and Other Essays

The Schools Our Children Deserve: Moving Beyond Traditional Classrooms and "Tougher Standards"

The Case Against Standardized Testing: Raising the Scores, Ruining the Schools

What Does It Mean to Be Well Educated?

Be Well Educated?

And More Essays on Standards, Grading, and Other Follies

Alfie Kohn

Beacon Press, Boston BEACON 150

BEACON PRESS
25 Beacon Street
Boston, Massachusetts 02108-2892
www.beacon.org

Beacon Press books
are published under the auspices of
the Unitarian Universalist Association of Congregations.

10 09 08   9 8 7 6

This book is printed on acid-free paper that meets the uncoated paper ANSI/NISO specifications for permanence as revised in 1992.

Composition by Wilsted & Taylor Publishing Services

LIBRARY OF CONGRESS CATALOGING-IN-PUBLICATION DATA

Kohn, Alfie.
  What does it mean to be well educated? and more essays on standards, grading, and other follies / Alfie Kohn.
      p. cm.
Includes bibliographical references and index.
  ISBN 0-8070-3267-0 (pbk. : alk. paper)
  1. Education—Aims and objectives—United States. I. Title.
LA217.2.K65 2004
370´.973—dc22   2003020744

Contents

Preface vii

Introduction: Grappling with Goals ix

One: The Purposes of Schooling

1. What Does It Mean to Be Well Educated? 1
2. Turning Learning into a Business 11
3. The Costs of Overemphasizing Achievement 28

Two: Standards and Testing

4. Confusing Harder with Better 41
5. Beware of the Standards, Not Just the Tests 46
6. Standardized Testing and Its Victims 54
7. Sacrificing Learning for Higher Scores 62
8. Two Cheers for an End to the SAT 65

Three: Grading and Evaluating

9. From Degrading to De-Grading 75
10. The Dangerous Myth of Grade Inflation 93
11. Five Reasons to Stop Saying "Good Job!" 106

Four: Moral, Social, and Psychological Questions

12. Constant Frustration and Occasional Violence: The Legacy of American High Schools 117
13. September 11 128
14. A Fresh Look at Abraham Maslow 131

Five: School Reform and the Study of Education

15. Almost There, But Not Quite 151
16. Education's Rotten Apples 159
17. The Folly of Merit Pay 166
18. Professors Who Profess 174

Credits 185
Index 188

Preface

The eighteen articles in this book, all originally published between 1999 and 2003, represent a fairly wide range in terms of length and style. At one end: a short, punchy op-ed for *USA Today* that lists just a few of the ways by which schools have suffered due to the desperate quest to raise test scores. At the other end: a long, not-so-punchy reassessment of Abraham Maslow's psychological theories, written for a book about humanistic psychology and education. In between: essays that appeared in twelve periodicals variously intended for teachers of young children, high school administrators, school board members, and university faculty members, among others.

During the five-year period in which these articles were written, I published two books dealing with what I take to be the most urgent educational issue of our time, namely the threat posed by the current "accountability" fad, with its undemocratic reliance on top-down standards and high-stakes testing. Naturally these issues are also addressed in a number of the articles from this period. But you'll find some reflections on very different questions as well, including the difficulty of changing classroom practice, the problem with praise, and what lessons we might draw from two tragic events: the shooting at Columbine High School and the attack on New York City and Washington that is now referred to simply by the date on which it occurred.

Because these essays appeared in different publications, their styles are not exactly consistent. In particular, you may notice that some of them contain bibliographies, some contain reference information in endnotes, and some contain no citations at all. I feel bad about those in the last category, although not quite bad enough to go to the trouble of inserting all the missing citations. If you're curious about a study that is described but not identified, write to me at my website (www.alfiekohn.org) and I'll do my best to dig up the information for you.

This book exists mostly because of the interest that Andrew Hrycyna at Beacon Press took in the project. Even more impressive than his enthusiasm, though, are his patience and professionalism, his shrewd judgment, and the graciousness he displayed during our disagreements about various editorial matters. Because we were in touch mostly by e-mail (despite the fact that we live in the same city), it was possible for me to communicate with him frequently, at great length, and about many issues, even though I remain unsure about how to pronounce his name. In any case, the book is much better in every way as a result of his editorial guidance.

Introduction: Grappling with Goals

I just about fell off my desk chair the other day when I came across my own name in an essay by a conservative economist who specializes in educational issues. The reason for my astonishment is that I was described as being "dead set against any fundamental changes in the nation's schools." Now, having been accused with some regularity of arguing for too damn many fundamental changes in the nation's schools, I found this new criticism more than a bit puzzling. But then I remembered that, during a TV interview a couple of years earlier, another author from a different right-wing think tank had labeled me a "defender of the educational status quo."

In an earlier age, I might have suggested pistols at dawn as the only fitting response to these calumnies. But of course there's a lot more going on here than the fact that one writer has had his radical credentials unjustly called into question. The point is that the mantle of school reform has been appropriated by those who oppose the whole idea of public schooling—and, as a rule, strongly support standardized testing. Their aim is to paint themselves as bold challengers of the current system and to claim that defenders of public education (as well as opponents of high-stakes tests) lack the vision or courage to endorse meaningful change. This rhetorical assault seemed to come out of nowhere, as though a memo had been circulated one day among those on the right: "Attention. Effective immediately, all of our efforts to privatize the schools will be known as 'reform,' and any opposition to those efforts will be known as 'anti-reform.' That is all."

Silver-lining hunters may note that this strategy pays a backhanded compliment to the idea of change. It implicitly acknowledges the inadequacy of conservatism, at least in the original sense of that word. These days everyone insists there's a problem with the way things are.[1] But it does no service to the clarity of language when self-described reformers have actually come to bury a given institution rather than to improve it. Widely publicized calls to "reform" environmental laws sometimes turn out to be efforts to water them down or even wash them away. And just ask someone who depends on public assistance what "welfare reform" really means.

It's not surprising that this PR strategy extends beyond schools, because so does the substance of what is being billed as reform. Efforts to dismantle public education are part of a much broader political movement whose patron saints are Milton Friedman and Ronald Reagan. The privatizers and deregulators already have notches in their belts for health care, prisons, banks, airlines, and electric utilities (say, *that's* been going well, hasn't it?). Now they're setting their sights on Social Security. I was recently reading about the added misery suffered by desperately poor families in various parts of the world as a result of the privatization of local water supplies.

In the case of education, people with an animus against public schools typically set the stage for their demolition plans by proclaiming that there isn't much worth saving. An impossible series of federal requirements for raising test scores—not for improving learning, mind you—is made-to-order for those who can then point to the predictably widespread "failures" as justification for abandoning the entire experiment of democratic public education. Meanwhile, those who object to these plans are portrayed as apologists for every policy in every school. It's a very clever gambit, you have to admit. Either you're in favor of privatization or else you are inexplicably satisfied with mediocrity.

But, wait! you sputter. Test scores tell you little more than which schools are located in affluent areas and which students have had to spend time preparing for these tests! Anyway, these are loaded dice you're playing with: The results are guaranteed to make the schools look bad! Plus, real reform doesn't entail turning our schools over to private corporations! And, sure, there are plenty of problems with American education, but what you're proposing will just make them worse!

What's that you say? You're *against reform?*

It's particularly difficult to address the issue of problems with American education in a sound bite. There's quite a bit to criticize about our schools: the way conformity is valued over curiosity and enforced with rewards and punishments, the way children are forced to compete against one another, the way meaning so often takes a back seat to skills in the curriculum, the way students are prevented from designing their own learning, the way instruction (not to mention assessment) is standardized, the way different avenues of study are rarely integrated, the way educators are systematically deskilled . . . And I'm just getting warmed up.

But not one of these defects will be corrected by privatizing schools. If anything, the micro-level effects (on teaching and learning) of this macro-level shift are likely to be counterproductive. Making schools resemble businesses often results in a kind of pedagogy that's not merely conservative but reactionary, turning back the clock on the few changes that have managed to infiltrate and improve our schools. Consider the back-to-basics philosophy, including stultifyingly scripted lessons, that pervades for-profit charter schools. Or have a look at some research from England showing that "when schools have to compete for students, they tend to adopt 'safe,' conventional and teacher-centered methods, to stay close to the prescribed curriculum, and to tailor teaching closely to test-taking."[2] (One more example of how competition undermines excellence.)

I am among those who think we should preserve but completely reimagine public education, a process John Goodlad likes to call school "renewal" rather than reform. As you'll see, this book offers a number of suggestions about where the status quo could use some serious reimagining. But to equate privatization with real reform distracts us from that endeavor, and indeed even from *talking* about where the problems lie and what sorts of changes we really need. Instead, it collapses the complex, multi-faceted questions about how to improve schools into a single dispute about whether they are to remain public. Thus do we become a nation at risk of failing to talk meaningfully about goals and practices.

Especially goals. In this book's final chapter, I observe that schools of education almost always offer a course on Methods but almost never a course on Goals. That's why I was delighted when a magazine editor invited me, among others, to try to un-pack the question of how we know when education has been successful. (My response appears as chapter 1, this book's title essay.) Questions like that aren't asked nearly enough. Rather, by default, we tend to pursue more limited—and limiting—objectives. And we do so without much attention to what we're doing, or what else we could be doing. For example, many of the practices associated with what now passes for school reform are commended to us on the grounds that they "raise standards." But no one should be satisfied with a phrase like that. What exactly does it mean, apart from making things more difficult for students (chapter 4) or preparing them to do better on standardized tests (chapter 6)? And what ultimate goals underlie *those* objectives? The fact is we rarely even bother to ask such questions.

The thing about goals, though, is that the failure to think or talk about them doesn't mean they're not there. Show me a school whose faculty defends doing "whatever works" and I'll show you a place tacitly defined by behaviorism. For complicated

reasons, the perspective of Thorndike, Skinner, and their descen-
dants—focusing exclusively on behaviors; conceiving of learning
as the transmission of discrete skills; controlling people with
reinforcers; and measuring, measuring, measuring—tends to be
accepted by default. Often, the absence of deliberate reflection
about educational goals results in a set of de facto goals that
are unambitious and uncontroversial, such as making your way
through a prescribed curriculum, making the kids do what
they're told, and making it to the weekend without incident.

If you're in a sailboat without a map or a destination, you can
get up to a good speed, but only in the direction that the prevailing winds are blowing. And who ultimately benefits from that?
Whose interests are served when, for lack of active conversation
about the direction in which we want to travel, we fall back on
just getting the students to show up, sit down, and swallow a list
of facts about minerals or modifiers or monarchies? Could it be
that more ambitious goals, including graduating a generation of
assertive critical thinkers, might not be to everyone's liking?

Not being a big fan of the prevailing winds, I think it's important to acknowledge where they're taking us and where we
might like to go instead. That's probably why (as my editor keeps
pointing out to me) all the essays in this collection are really
about goals—even the ones that don't seem to be. In many cases,
my purpose is to argue about the value of one objective as opposed to another. But sometimes I have a more modest aim—
namely, asking whether people's practices are even consistent
with their own goals. I told an interviewer recently that much of
what I do for a living is to say, to different audiences and about
different topics, "You seem to want this. So how come you're doing that?" Calling attention to a discrepancy between people's
objectives and their actions invites them to begin to question
those actions. Never mind that *I* don't like grades: What matters

is that *you* want kids to be excited about what they're learning, and the research strongly suggests that that's less likely to happen when students are led to focus on getting A's (chapter 9).

The trick, however, when deciding what we really want, is to look beyond the surface and think past the short term. This morning, a teacher's primary concern for her students may be for them to solve a batch of long-division problems correctly. But how does that immediate goal (and the practices associated with it) square with such long-term objectives as wanting them to understand quantitative concepts from the inside out, to be proficient and engaged and maybe even to get a kick out of playing around with numbers? And how do our goals for these kids in these subjects comport with even broader questions about the purposes of schooling?

If you prefer, we can work backward—as do several of the essays in this book: Start with what we're looking for and then ask what kinds of classrooms we need to construct. What sorts of teaching are most likely to produce a particular set of results—and, equally important, what sorts of teaching are likely to get in the way (chapter 16)? Once you conclude that schools should meet the developmental needs of the children who attend them instead of just forcing children to adapt to the needs of the institution, what implications does that have for the kind of education we offer to, say, teenagers (chapter 12)? Once you've decided you want students to take satisfaction from their own accomplishments rather than to become dependent on the approval of authority figures, how does that affect the way you respond to their successes (chapter 11)? Once you're pretty sure you'd like your kids to realize that the life of someone who lives in Kabul or Baghdad is worth no less than the life of someone from their own neighborhood, what does that do to your social studies curriculum or your approach to character education (chapter 13)? There are why's worth pondering beneath all the how's: To pose sharp questions about strategy obligates us to grapple with goals.

For readers whose point of departure is a worldview very different from my own, my objective, naturally, is to invite them to look at things a little differently by the end of an essay than they did at the beginning. But for everyone else, my hope is to provoke reconsideration of practices, and even of goals, by beginning with the basic values we share. That's what allows a logical progression of reappraisal: Given that we're agreed on this broad (or long-term) principle, how much sense does it make to pursue these narrow (or short-term) goals, and then, in consequence, how wise are these policies and behaviors?

Such questioning can take place as a national dialogue, a concerted and deliberate invitation for all of us to reflect on the proper purposes of education. But it also can take place in a school parking lot as two or three teachers linger for a few minutes to chat about what the point is of having students read a certain book or follow a certain rule. Private conversations are fine—as long as they're about how to nourish our public schools.

Notes

1. On one level, this posture is familiar: Polemicists across the political spectrum frequently try to describe whatever position they're about to criticize as "fashionable." The implication is that only the bravest soul—that is, the writer—dares to support an unfashionable view.

2. Kari Delhi, "Shopping for Schools," *Orbit* (published by the Ontario Institute for Studies in Education at the University of Toronto), vol. 25, no. 1 (1998): 32. The author cites three studies from the U.K. in support of this conclusion.

One: The Purposes of Schooling

1. What Does It Mean to Be Well Educated?

No one should offer pronouncements about what it means to be well educated without meeting my wife. When I met Alisa, she was at Harvard, putting the finishing touches on her doctoral dissertation in anthropology. A year later, having spent her entire life in school, she decided to do the only logical thing . . . and apply to medical school. Today she is a practicing physician—and an excellent one at that, judging by feedback from her patients and colleagues.

She will, however, freeze up if you ask her what eight times seven is, because she never learned the multiplication table. And forget about grammar ("Me and him went over her house today" is fairly typical) or literature ("Who's Faulkner?"). After a dozen years, I continue to be impressed on a regular basis by the agility of her mind as well as by how much she doesn't know. (I'm also bowled over by what a wonderful person she is, but that's beside the point.)

So what do you make of this paradox with whom I live? Is she a walking indictment of the system that let her get so far—twenty-nine years of schooling, not counting medical residency—without acquiring the basics of English and math? Or does she offer an invitation to rethink what it means to be well educated since what she lacks hasn't prevented her from being a deep-thinking, high-functioning, multiply credentialed, professionally successful individual?

Of course, if those features describe what it means to be well educated, then there is no dilemma to be resolved. She fits the bill. The problem arises only if your definition includes a list of facts and skills that one must have but that she lacks. In that case,

Originally published in *Principal Leadership* in 2003.

though, my wife is not alone. Thanks to the Internet, which allows writers and researchers to circulate rough drafts of their manuscripts, I've come to realize just how many truly brilliant people cannot spell or punctuate. Their insights and discoveries may be changing the shape of their respective fields, but they can't use an apostrophe correctly to save their lives.

Or what about me (he suddenly inquired, relinquishing the comfortable perch from which issue all those judgments of other people)? I could embarrass myself pretty quickly by listing the number of classic works of literature I've never read. And I can multiply reasonably well, but everything mathematical I was taught after first-year algebra (and even some of that) is completely gone. How well educated am I?

The issue is sufficiently complex that questions are easier to formulate than answers. So let's at least be sure we're asking the right questions and framing them well.

1. The Point of Schooling: Rather than attempting to define what it means to be well educated, should we instead be asking about the *purposes of education?* The latter formulation invites us to look beyond academic goals. For example, Nel Noddings, professor emerita at Stanford University, urges us to reject "the deadly notion that the schools' first priority should be intellectual development" and contends that "the main aim of education should be to produce competent, caring, loving, and lovable people." Alternatively, we might wade into the dispute between those who see education as a means to creating or sustaining a democratic society and those who believe its primary role is economic, amounting to an "investment" in future workers and, ultimately, corporate profits. In short, perhaps the question "How do we know if education has been successful?" shouldn't be posed until we have asked what it's supposed to be successful *at*.

2. Evaluating People vs. Their Education: Does the phrase *well educated* refer to a quality of the schooling you received, or to something about you? Does it denote what you were taught, or what you learned (and remember)? If the term applies to what you now know and can do, you could be poorly educated despite having received a top-notch education. However, if the term refers to the quality of your schooling, then we'd have to conclude that a lot of "well-educated" people sat through lessons that barely registered, or at least are hazy to the point of irrelevance a few years later.

3. An Absence of Consensus: Is it even possible to agree on *a single definition* of what every high school student should know or be able to do in order to be considered well educated? Is such a definition expected to remain invariant across cultures (with a single standard for the United States and Somalia, for example), or even across subcultures (South-Central Los Angeles and Scarsdale; a Louisiana fishing community, the Upper East Side of Manhattan, and Pennsylvania Dutch country)? How about across historical eras: Would anyone seriously argue that our criteria for "well educated" today are exactly the same as those used a century ago—or that they should be?

To cast a skeptical eye on such claims is not necessarily to suggest that the term is purely relativistic: You like vanilla, I like chocolate; you favor knowledge about poetry, I prefer familiarity with the Gettysburg Address. Some criteria are more defensible than others. Nevertheless, we have to acknowledge a striking absence of consensus about what the term ought to mean. Furthermore, any consensus that does develop is ineluctably rooted in time and place. It is misleading and even dangerous to justify our own pedagogical values by pretending they are grounded in some objective, transcendent Truth, as though the quality of being well educated is a Platonic form waiting to be discovered.

4. Some Poor Definitions: Should we instead try to stipulate which answers *don't* make sense? I'd argue that certain attributes are either insufficient (possessing them isn't enough to make one well educated) or unnecessary (one can be well educated without possessing them)—or both. Let us therefore consider ruling out:

Seat time. Merely sitting in classrooms for *x* hours doesn't make one well educated.

Job skills. It would be a mistake to reduce schooling to vocational preparation, if only because we can easily imagine graduates who are well prepared for the workplace (or at least for some workplaces) but whom we would not regard as well educated. In any case, pressure to redesign secondary education so as to suit the demands of employers reflects little more than the financial interests—and the political power—of these corporations.

Test scores. To a disconcerting extent, high scores on standardized tests signify a facility with taking standardized tests. Most teachers can instantly name students who are talented thinkers but who just don't do well on these exams—as well as students whose scores seem to *over*estimate their intellectual gifts. Indeed, researchers have found a statistically significant correlation between high scores on a range of standardized tests and a shallow approach to learning. In any case, no single test is sufficiently valid, reliable, or meaningful that it can be treated as a marker for academic success.

Memorization of a bunch o' facts. Familiarity with a list of words, names, books, and ideas is a uniquely poor way to judge who is well educated. As the philosopher Alfred North Whitehead observed long ago, "A merely well-informed man is the most useless bore on God's earth." "Scraps of information" are worth something only if they are put to use, or at least "thrown into fresh combinations."

Look more carefully at the superficially plausible claim that you must be familiar with, say, *King Lear* in order to be considered well educated. To be sure, it's a classic meditation on mortality, greed, belated understanding, and other important themes. But *how* familiar with it must you be? Is it enough that you can name its author, or that you know it's a play? Do you have to be able to recite the basic plot? What if you read it once but barely remember it now?

If you don't like that example, pick another one. How much do you have to know about neutrinos, or the Boxer rebellion, or the side-angle-side theorem? If deep understanding is required, then (a) very few people could be considered well educated (which raises serious doubts about the reasonableness of such a definition), and (b) the number of items about which anyone could have that level of knowledge is sharply limited because time is finite. On the other hand, how can we justify a cocktail-party level of familiarity with all these items—reminiscent of Woody Allen's summary of *War and Peace* after taking a speed-reading course: "It's about Russia." What sense does it make to say that one person is well educated for having a single sentence's worth of knowledge about the Progressive Era or photosynthesis, while someone who has to look it up is not?

Knowing a lot of stuff may seem harmless, albeit insufficient, but the problem is that efforts to shape schooling around this goal, dressed up with pretentious labels like "cultural literacy," have the effect of taking time away from more meaningful objectives, such as knowing how to think. If the Bunch o' Facts model proves a poor foundation on which to decide who is properly educated, it makes no sense to peel off items from such a list and assign clusters of them to students at each grade level. It is as poor a basis for designing curriculum as it is for judging the success of schooling.

The number of people who do, in fact, confuse the possession of a storehouse of knowledge with being "smart"—the latter being a disconcertingly common designation for those who fare well on quiz shows—is testament to the naive appeal that such a model holds. But there are also political implications to be considered here. To emphasize the importance of absorbing a pile of information is to support a larger worldview that sees the primary purpose of education as reproducing our current culture. It is probably not a coincidence that a Core Knowledge model wins rave reviews from Phyllis Schlafly's Eagle Forum (and other conservative Christian groups) as well as from the likes of *Investor's Business Daily*. To be sure, not every individual who favors this approach is a right-winger, but defining the notion of educational mastery in terms of the number of facts one can recall is well suited to the task of preserving the status quo. By contrast, consider Dewey's suggestion that an educated person is one who has "gained the power of reflective attention, the power to hold problems, questions, before the mind." Without this capability, he added, "the mind remains at the mercy of custom and external suggestions."

5. Mandating a Single Definition: *Who gets to decide* what it means to be well educated? Even assuming that you and I agree to include one criterion and exclude another, that doesn't mean our definition should be imposed with the force of law—taking the form, for example, of requirements for a high school diploma. There are other considerations, such as the real suffering imposed on individuals who aren't permitted to graduate from high school, the egregious disparities in resources and opportunities available in different neighborhoods, and so on.

More to the point, the fact that so many of us *don't* agree suggests that a national (or, better yet, international) conversation should continue, that one definition may never fit all, and, therefore, that we should leave it up to local communities to decide who gets to graduate. But that is not what has happened. In about half the states, people sitting atop Mount Olympus have decreed that anyone who doesn't pass a certain standardized test will be denied a diploma and, by implication, classified as inadequately educated. This example of accountability gone haywire violates not only common sense but the consensus of educational measurement specialists. And the consequences are entirely predictable: no high school graduation for a disproportionate number of students of color, from low-income neighborhoods, with learning disabilities, attending vocational schools, or not yet fluent in English.

Less obviously, the idea of making diplomas contingent on passing an exam answers by default the question of what it means to be well (or sufficiently) educated: Rather than grappling with the messy issues involved, we simply declare that standardized tests will tell us the answer. This is disturbing not merely because of the inherent limits of the tests, but also because teaching becomes distorted when passing those tests becomes the paramount goal. Students arguably receive an inferior education when pressure is applied to raise their test scores, which means that high school exit exams may actually *lower* standards.

Beyond proclaiming "Pass this standardized test or you don't graduate," most states now issue long lists of curriculum standards, containing hundreds of facts, skills, and subskills that all students are expected to master at a given grade level and for a given subject. These standards are not guidelines but mandates (to which teachers are supposed to "align" their instruction). In effect, a Core Knowledge model, with its implication of students as interchangeable receptacles into which knowledge is poured, has become the law of the land in many places. Surely even defenders of this approach can appreciate the difference between *arguing* in its behalf and *requiring* that every school adopt it.

6. The Good School: Finally, instead of asking what it means to be well educated, perhaps we should inquire into the *qualities of a school* likely to offer a good education. I've offered my own answer to that question at book length, as have others. As I see it, the best sort of schooling is organized around problems, projects, and questions—as opposed to facts, skills, and disciplines. Knowledge is acquired, of course, but in a context and for a purpose. The emphasis is not only on depth rather than breadth, but also on discovering ideas rather than on covering a prescribed curriculum. Teachers are generalists first and specialists (in a given subject matter) second; they commonly collaborate to offer interdisciplinary courses that students play an active role in designing. All of this happens in small, democratic schools that are experienced as caring communities.

Notwithstanding the claims of traditionalists eager to offer —and then dismiss—a touchy-feely caricature of progressive education, a substantial body of evidence exists to support the effectiveness of each of these components as well as the benefits of using them in combination. By contrast, it isn't easy to find *any* data to justify the traditional (and still dominant) model of secondary education: large schools, short classes, huge student loads for each teacher, a fact-transmission kind of instruction that is the very antithesis of "student-centered," the virtual absence of any attempt to integrate diverse areas of study, the rating and ranking of students, and so on. Such a system acts as a powerful *obstacle* to good teaching, and it thwarts the best efforts of many talented educators on a daily basis.

Low-quality instruction can be assessed with low-quality tests, including homegrown quizzes and standardized exams designed to measure (with faux objectivity) the number of facts and skills crammed into short-term memory. The effects of high-quality instruction are trickier, but not impossible, to assess. The most promising model turns on the notion of "exhibitions" of learning, in which students reveal their understanding by means of in-depth projects, portfolios of assignments, and other demonstrations—a model pioneered by Ted Sizer, Deborah Meier, and others affiliated with the Coalition of Essential Schools. By now we're fortunate to have access not only to essays about how this might be done (such as Sizer's invaluable *Horace* series) but to books about schools that are actually doing it: *The Power of Their Ideas* by Meier, about Central Park East Secondary School in New York City; *Rethinking High School* by Harvey Daniels and his colleagues, about Best Practice High School in Chicago; and *One Kid at a Time* by Eliot Levine, about the Met in Providence, Rhode Island.

The assessments in such schools are based on meaningful standards of excellence, standards that may collectively offer the best answer to our original question simply because to meet those criteria is as good a way as any to show that one is well educated. The Met School focuses on social reasoning, empirical reasoning, quantitative reasoning, communication, and personal qualities (such as responsibility, capacity for leadership, and self-awareness). Meier has emphasized the importance of developing five "habits of mind": the value of raising questions about *evidence* ("How do we know what we know?"), *point of view* ("Whose perspective does this represent?"), *connections* ("How is this related to that?"), *supposition* ("How might things have been otherwise?"), and *relevance* ("Why is this important?").

It's not only the ability to raise and answer those questions that matters, though, but also the disposition to do so. For that matter, any set of intellectual objectives, any description of what it means to think deeply and critically, should be accompanied by a reference to one's *interest* or intrinsic motivation to do such thinking. Dewey reminded us that the goal of education is more education. To be well educated, then, is to have the desire as well as the means to make sure that learning never ends.

2. Turning Learning into a Business

The best reason to give a child a good school . . . is so that child will have a happy childhood, and not so that it will help IBM in competing with Sony . . . There is something ethically embarrassing about resting a national agenda on the basis of sheer greed.

—JONATHAN KOZOL

I give a lot of speeches these days about the accountability fad that has been turning our schools into glorified test-prep centers. The question-and-answer sessions that follow these lectures can veer off in unexpected directions, but it is increasingly likely that someone will inquire about the darker forces behind this heavy-handed version of school reform. Aren't giant corporations raking in profits from standardized testing? a questioner will demand. Doesn't it stand to reason that these companies engineered the reliance on testing in the first place?

Indeed, there are enough suspicious connections to keep conspiracy theorists awake through the night. For example, Standard & Poors, the financial rating service, has lately been offering to evaluate and publish the performance, based largely on test scores, of every school district in a given state—a bit of number crunching that Michigan and Pennsylvania purchased for at least $10 million each, and other states may soon follow. The explicit findings of these reports concern whether this district is doing better than that one. But the tacit message—the hidden curriculum, if you will—is that test scores are a useful and appropriate marker for school quality. Who has an incentive to convince people of that conclusion? Well, it turns out that Standard & Poors is owned by McGraw-Hill, one of the largest manufacturers of standardized tests.

With such pressure to look good by boosting their test results,

Originally published in *Phi Delta Kappan* in 2002.

low-scoring districts may feel compelled to purchase heavily scripted curriculum programs designed to raise scores, programs such as Open Court or Reading Mastery (and others in the Direct Instruction series). Where do those programs come from? By an astonishing coincidence, both are owned by McGraw-Hill. Of course, it doesn't hurt to have some influential policymakers on your side when it's time to make choices about curriculum and assessment. In April 2000, Charlotte K. Frank joined the state of New York's top education policymaking panel, the Board of Regents. If you need to reach Ms. Frank, try her office at McGraw-Hill, where she is a vice president. And we needn't even explore the chummy relationship between Harold McGraw III (the company's chairman) and George W. Bush.[1] Nor will we investigate the strong statement of support for test-based accountability in a *Business Week* cover story about education published in March 2001. Care to guess what company owns *Business Week?*

Stumble across enough suspicious relationships like these and your eyebrows may never come down. However, we don't want to oversimplify. The sizable profits made by the CTB division of McGraw-Hill, as well as by Harcourt Educational Measurement, Riverside Publishing, Educational Testing Service (ETS), and NCS Pearson[2]—the five companies that develop and/or score virtually all the standardized tests to which students and prospective teachers are subjected—cannot completely explain why public officials, journalists, and others have come to rely so heavily on these exams. Let's face it: For a variety of reasons, people with no financial stake in the matter have become boosters of standardized testing.[3]

More important, even if one could point to a neat cause-and-effect relationship here, the role that business plays in education is not limited to the realm of testing. Indeed, its influence is even deeper, more complicated, and ultimately more disturbing than anything we might reveal in a game of connect the corporate dots. Schools—and, by extension, children—have been turned into sources of profit in several distinct ways. Yes, some corporations sell educational products, including tests, texts, and other curriculum materials. But many more corporations, peddling all sorts of products, have come to see schools as places to reach an enormous captive market. Advertisements are posted in cafeterias, athletic fields, even on buses. Soft-drink companies pay off schools so that their brand, and only their brand, of liquid candy will be sold to kids.[4] Schools are offered free televisions in exchange for compelling students to watch a brief current-events program larded with commercials, a project known as Channel One. (The advertisers seem to be getting their money's worth: Researchers have found that Channel One viewers, as contrasted with a comparison group of students, not only thought more highly of products advertised on the program but were more likely to agree with statements such as "money is everything," "a nice car is more important than school," "designer labels make a difference," and "I want what I see advertised.")[5]

Even more disturbing than having public schools sanction and expose children to advertisements[6] is the fact that corporate propaganda is sometimes passed off as part of the curriculum. Math problems plug a particular brand of sneakers or candy; chemical companies distribute slick curriculum packages to ensure that environmental science will be taught with their slant.[7] A few years ago, someone sent me a large, colorful brochure aimed at educators that touts several free lessons helpfully supplied by Procter & Gamble. One kit helps fifth-graders learn about personal hygiene by way of Old Spice aftershave and Secret deodorant, while another promises a seventh-grade lesson on the "ten steps to self-esteem," complete with teacher's guide, video, and samples of Clearasil.

It's worth thinking about how corporate sponsorship is likely to affect what is included—and not included—in these lessons. How likely is it that the makers of Clearasil would emphasize that how you feel about yourself should not primarily be a function of how you look? Or consider a hypothetical unit on nutrition underwritten by Kraft General Foods (or by McDonald's or Coca-Cola): Would you expect to find any mention of the fact that the food you prepare yourself is likely to be more nutritious than processed products in boxes and jars and cans? Or that the best way to quench your thirst is actually to drink water? Or that a well-balanced diet requires little or no meat? Or that smoking causes cancer? (Kraft General Foods—and Nabisco, for that matter—is owned by a tobacco company.)

A few companies, then, make money by selling books and tests, while many more sell other things to children. The third, and most audacious, way that schooling can be milked for profit is by letting corporations take over the management of the schools themselves, or even allowing them to own schools outright as they would a car dealership. Opportunities for such businesses have greatly expanded as a result of a movement simply to privatize education. This effort seems to gather strength as people friendly to its aims find themselves in positions of power, as the Supreme Court narrowly voted in June 2002 to allow public funds to pay for tuition at private—including religious —schools, and as proponents become more skilled at public relations (for example, jettisoning the unpopular word *vouchers* and justifying their agenda in terms of its ostensible benefits for low-income people of color).

By way of background, consider that the center of gravity for American education has shifted over the last few years from local schools and districts to state capitals. The commissioner or state superintendent of schools, the state board of education, and the legislature have usurped much of the power that communities have long enjoyed to set education policy. Indeed, even Washington, D.C. has gotten into the act, with new federal legislation requiring that every state test every student every year. It's understandable, then, that frustrated students, parents, and teachers would be inclined to see government as the problem. Some conservative activists have even begun referring derisively to public schools as "government schools." But there are two problems with this equation. First, the current level of interference in curricular and assessment decisions by politicians is not logically entailed by the idea of public schooling; indeed, it is unprecedented. If your governor began telling your local library which books to order, that would not be an argument against the idea of public libraries. Second, the actions taken by government officials have been offensive precisely to the extent that they have appropriated the slogans and mindset of private enterprise. The problem is that people in the public sector are uncritically adopting the worldview of the private sector—and applying it to schools.

Privatizing education is predicated on an almost childlike faith in competition: Let self-interested people struggle against one another, and somehow all of them—even their children, presumably—will benefit. This belief, as quickly becomes evident from reading and listening to those who hold it, has the status of religious dogma rather than empirical hypothesis. It is closely related to a second ideological underpinning: a pronounced individualism in which there is no us, just you and her and him and me. To apply a marketplace mentality to education both assumes and exacerbates this perspective, with parents encouraged to focus only on what improves their own children's position. This is the very opposite of an invitation to work together to make schools more effective and inviting places for all our children. Perhaps it was the implications of this threat to the value of community that led the political philosopher Benjamin Barber to observe, "Privatization is not about limiting government; it is about terminating democracy."

Clearly, education is just one arena in which larger ideologies are being played out. These days, as education historian David Labaree put it, "We find public schools under attack, not just because they are deemed ineffective, but because they are public."[8] Once the struggle over public institutions has been joined in the classroom, though, it isn't hard to understand the consequences of implementing voucher plans and other "school choice" proposals—including, to some extent, charter schools, which many see as a first step toward undermining public schooling altogether. What happens to schools when they are plunged into the marketplace? To begin with, they must shift much of their time and resources to, well, marketing. (It is those who sell themselves skillfully, not those who are especially good at what they do, who tend to succeed in a competitive market.) Moreover, the pressure to make themselves look better presents a temptation to screen out less desirable students, those whose education takes more effort or expense. "The problem with public schools," remarked author John Chubb, "is that they must take whoever walks in the door."[9] The philosophical core of the privatization movement for which Chubb speaks is neatly revealed in the use of the word *problem* in that sentence.

Deborah Meier writes memorably of the "dictatorship of the marketplace," noting that "privatizing removes schools from democratic control." She observes that private schools "cannot serve as general models; their value and advantages depend on their scarcity . . . Schools dependent upon private clienteles—schools that can get rid of unwanted kids or troublemaker families . . . and toss aside the losers—not only can avoid the democratic arts of compromise and tolerance but also implicitly foster lessons about the power of money and prestige, a lesson already too well known by every adolescent in America."[10] Meier's indictment extends beyond voucher programs, suggesting the corrosive effect of any sort of interference in public education by business interests. The quest for private profits, in whatever form it takes, can only contaminate efforts to help all students become enthusiastic and expert learners.

These three basic ways by which corporations can profit from education are all quite straightforward. Houghton Mifflin, which owns Riverside, makes money selling the Iowa Test of Basic Skills. Nike makes money by advertising its shoes to young people who are required by law to be in the vicinity of its billboards. Edison, Inc. makes money (or will do so eventually, it assures its investors) by running whole schools.

But there are also more indirect ways to turn learning into a business. When corporations can influence the nature of curriculum and the philosophy of education, then they have succeeded in doing something more profound, and possibly more enduring, than merely improving their results on this quarter's balance sheet. That can happen when businesses succeed in creating "school-to-work" programs, by which children are defined as future workers and shaped to the specifications of their employers. It can happen when the whole notion of education as a public good is systematically undermined—an ideological shift that paves the way for privatizing schools. It can happen when a business ethos takes over education, with an emphasis on quantifiable results, on standardized procedures to improve performance, on order and discipline and obedience to authority. Students expect to be controlled with rewards and punishments, to be set against their peers in competitions, to be rated and evaluated by those who have more power than they do. None of this is particularly effective at preparing children to be critical thinkers, lifelong intellectual explorers, active participants in a democratic society—or even, for that matter, good friends or lovers or parents. But the process is exceedingly effective at preparing them for their life as corporate employees.

Rather ingeniously, some practices serve the interests of business in multiple ways simultaneously. For example, selling products in classrooms may immediately increase a company's market share, but it also contributes to a socialization process whereby children come to see themselves as consumers, as people whose lives will be improved by buying more things.

Standardized testing may be an even better illustration in that it manages to achieve several goals at one stroke:

• it brings in hundreds of millions of dollars a year to the handful of corporations that produce the tests, grade the tests, and supply materials to raise students' scores on the tests;

• it screens and sorts students for the convenience of industry (and higher education);

• it helps to foster acceptance of a corporate-style ideology, which comes to be seen as natural and even desirable, in which assessment is used less to support learning than to evaluate and compare people—and in which the education driven by that testing has a uniform, standardized feel to it; and finally

• when many students perform poorly on these tests (an outcome that can be ensured from the outset, and then justified in the name of "raising the bar"), these results can be used to promote discontent with public education: "We are shocked— shocked!—to discover just how bad our schools are!" Again, this can create a more receptive climate for introducing vouchers, for-profit charter schools, and other private alternatives. (Anyone whose goal was to serve up our schools to the marketplace could hardly find a shrewder strategy than to insist on holding schools "accountable" by administering wave after wave of standardized tests.)

To the extent that colleges, too, are increasingly seen as ripe for a corporate makeover, testing younger students would make sense as part of a long-term strategy. In the words of one instructor: "The whole standards movement, after all, is about restricting learning to what is *actually useful:* the memorization of information, the streamlining of knowledge to what can be evaluated by a standardized test. By curtailing the excessive autonomy of K–12 teachers and requiring them to teach 'to the tests,' we are preparing future college students for a brand of higher education designed and administered by the savviest segment of our society: for-profit corporations."[11]

There may be some sort of shadowy business conspiracy at work to turn schools into factories, but this seems unlikely if only because no such conspiracy is necessary to produce the desired results. Most politicians have uncritically accepted the goals and methods outlined by the private sector—and, with the possible exception of attitudes toward vouchers, there are few differences between the two major parties. Marveling that "Democrats and Republicans are saying rather similar things about education," a front-page story in the *New York Times* explained, "One reason there seems to be such a consensus on education is that the economic rationale for schooling has triumphed."[12]

More ominous is the extent to which even educators have internalized a business approach. Many of us defend "partnerships" between schools and businesses, willingly "align" our teaching to uniform state standards, shrug off objections to advertising in the schools, refer to learning as "work"[13] or schooling itself as an "investment." The next time you leaf through one of the leading education periodicals—or listen to a speech at a conference—try counting all the telltale signs of corporate ideology.

There's no need for executives in expensive suits to show up in schools if we're already doing their work for them.

Some readers may dismiss as rhetorical excess any comparison of schools with factories. In fact, though, the analogy was first proposed by people who were quite explicit about wanting to make the former more similar to the latter. Back in 1916, one Ellwood Cubberley wrote that "our schools are, in a sense, factories in which the raw products (children) are to be shaped and fashioned into products to meet the various demands of life."[14] In the 1950s, this way of thinking was still in favor. A *Fortune* magazine article titled "The Low Productivity of the Education Industry" informed readers that we should strive "to turn out students with the greatest possible efficiency . . . [and] minimize the input of man hours and capital. In this respect, the schools are no different from General Motors."[15]

The popularity of such parallels may wax and wane over time, but were Mr. Cubberley to find himself magically transported to the early twenty-first century, he would almost certainly feel right at home. He would immediately notice that thousands of American schools, some of them dating back to his own era but still open for, um, business, literally resemble factories. Inside them, he would see, as Linda Darling-Hammond observed in 1997, that "the short segmented tasks stressing speed and neatness that predominate in most schools, the emphasis on rules from the important to the trivial, and the obsession with bells, schedules, and time clocks are all dug deep into the ethos of late-nineteenth-century America, when students were being prepared to work in factories on predetermined tasks that would not require them to figure out what to do."[16]

Cubberley would likely be impressed as well by the remarkable power that business continues to have in shaping educational policy. Every few months, he would notice, another report on American schooling is released by a consortium of large corporations. These documents normally receive wide and approving press attention despite the fact that they all recycle the same set of buzzwords. Rather like a party game in which players create sentences by randomly selecting an adjective from one list, then a noun from another, these dispatches from the business world seem to consist mostly of different combinations of terms like *world-class, competitive,* and *measurable; standards, results,* and *accountability.*

A few examples from the last decade that might set Mr. Cubberley's head to nodding: The Committee for Economic Development, consisting of executives from about 250 large companies, demands that school curricula be linked more closely to employers' skill requirements; it calls for "performance-driven education," incentives, and a traditional "core disciplinary knowledge" version of instruction. Ditto for the Business Roundtable, which describes schooling as "competing in the education Olympics." Besides endorsing narrow and very specific academic standards, punishment for schools that fall behind, and more testing, it approvingly cites the example of taking time in high school to familiarize students with personnel evaluations. The National Association of Manufacturers, meanwhile, insists on more testing as well as "a national system of skills standards designed by industry." And the Business Task Force on Student Standards says that "workplace performance requirements of industry and commerce must be integrated into subject-matter standards and learning environments."[17]

To scan these recommendations is to realize two things. First, most have been adopted as policy. To an extraordinary degree, business's wish becomes education's command. Second, they traffic in the realm not only of methods and metaphors, but of purposes and goals. The question is not just whether we will compare schools to factories, or even whether we will prescribe practices that will make schools more like factories. The question is what vision of schooling—and even of children—lies behind such suggestions. While a proper discussion of the purpose of education lies outside the scope of this essay,[18] it is immediately evident that seeing schools as a means for bolstering our economic system (and the interests of the major players in that system) is very different from seeing education as a means for strengthening democracy, for promoting social justice, or simply for fostering the well-being and development of the students themselves.[19]

In the final analysis, the problem with letting business interests shape our country's educational agenda isn't just their lack of knowledge about the nuances of pedagogy. The problem is with their ultimate objectives. Corporations in our economic system exist to provide a financial return to the people who own them: They are in business to make a profit. As individuals, those who work in (or even run) these companies might have other goals, too, when they turn their attention to public policy or education or anything else. But business *qua* business is concerned principally about its own bottom line. Thus, when business thinks about schools, its agenda is driven by what will maximize its profitability, not necessarily by what is in the best interest of students. Any overlap between those two goals would be purely accidental—and, in practice, turns out to be minimal. What maximizes corporate profits often does not benefit children, and vice versa. Qualities such as a love of learning for its own sake, a penchant for asking challenging questions, or a commitment to democratic participation in decision making would be seen as nice but irrelevant—or perhaps even as impediments to the efficient realization of corporate goals.

Some people in the business world object to this characterization, of course. They insist that modern corporations have similar goals to those of educators, that business today needs employees who are critical thinkers and problem solvers skilled at teamwork, and so forth. But if this were really true, we would see cutting-edge companies taking the lead in demanding a constructivist approach to instruction, where students' questions drive the curriculum—as well as a rich, Whole Language model for teaching literacy. They would ask why we haven't thrown out the worksheets and the textbooks, the isolated skills and rote memorization. They would demand greater emphasis on cooperative learning and complain loudly about the practices that undermine collaboration (and ultimately quality)—practices like awards assemblies and spelling bees and honor rolls, or norm-referenced tests. They would insist on heterogeneous, inclusive classrooms in place of programs that segregate and stratify and stigmatize. They would stop talking about "school choice" (meaning programs that treat education as a commodity for sale) and start talking about the importance of giving students more choice about what happens in their classrooms. They would publish reports on the importance of turning schools into caring communities where mutual problem-solving replaces an emphasis on following directions.

The sad truth, of course, is that when business leaders do address these issues, their approach tends to be precisely the opposite: They write off innovative, progressive educational reforms as mere fads that distract us from raising test scores. This is evident not only from those reports sampled above (from the Business Roundtable and similar groups) but also from the consistent slant of articles about education that appear in business-oriented periodicals.

Moreover, while there may be more talk in boardrooms these days about teamwork, it is usually situated in the context of competitiveness—that is, working together so we can defeat another group of people working together. (Business groups commonly characterize students as competitors—as people who do, or will, or should spend their lives trying to beat other people. Other nations are likewise depicted as rivals, such that to make our schools "world class" means not that we should cooperate with other countries and learn, but that we should compete against them and win.) While "social skills" are often listed as desirable attributes, business publications never seem to mention such qualities as generosity or compassion. While it is common to talk about the need for future employees who can think critically, there is reason to doubt that corporate executives want people with the critical skills to ask why they (the executives) just received multimillion-dollar stock option packages even as several thousand employees were thrown out of work. Corporations may, as we have seen, encourage high school English teachers to assign students the task of writing a sample personnel evaluation, but they seem less keen on inviting students to critically analyze whether such evaluations make sense, or who gets to evaluate whom. In short, what business wants from its workers—and, by extension, from our schools—in the twenty-first century may not be so different after all from what it wanted in the twentieth and even nineteenth centuries.

What it wants, moreover, it usually gets. It doesn't take a degree in political science to figure out why politicians (and sometimes even educators) so often capitulate to business. For that matter, it isn't much of a mystery why a five-hundred-pound gorilla is invited to sleep anywhere it wishes. But that doesn't make the practice any less dangerous.

Indeed, we might even go so far as to identify as one of the most crucial tasks in a democratic society the act of limiting the power that corporations have in determining what happens in, and to, our schools. Not long ago, as historian Joel Spring pointed out, you would have been branded a radical (or worse) for suggesting that our educational system is geared to meeting the needs of business. Today, corporations not only acknowledge that fact but freely complain when they think schools aren't adequately meeting their needs. They are not shy about trying to make over the schools in their own image. It's up to the rest of us, therefore, to firmly tell them to mind their own businesses.

Notes

1. See Stephen Metcalf, "Reading Between the Lines," *The Nation,* January 28, 2002, pp. 18–22—reprinted in A. Kohn and P. Shannon, eds., *Education, Inc.: Turning Learning into a Business,* rev. ed. (Portsmouth, N.H.: Heinemann, 2002).

2. Notice that the phenomenon by which a company makes money by testing students, then turns around and sells the materials designed to prepare students for those tests, is not limited to McGraw-Hill. Many of the major textbook publishers are represented in this list of test manufacturers.

3. For other explanations, see Alfie Kohn, *The Case Against Standardized Testing* (Portsmouth, N.H.: Heinemann, 2000), esp. pp. 2–4; Robert L. Linn, "Assessments and Accountability," *Educational Researcher* (March 2000), esp. p. 4; and Gary Natriello and Aaron M. Pallas, "The Development and Impact of High-Stakes Testing," in *Raising Standards or Raising Barriers?,* edited by Gary Orfield and Mindy L. Kornhaber (New York: Century Foundation Press, 2001), esp. pp. 20–21.

4. See Alex Molnar, "Looking for Funds in All the Wrong Places," *Principal* (November 2000): 18–21. Thanks to Pat Shannon for calling this article to my attention. As of early 2002, between three and four hundred school districts had signed exclusive beverage contracts—more than double the number in mid-1999—according to the Center for Commercial-Free Public Education.

5. Bradley S. Greenberg and Jeffrey E. Brand, "Channel One: But What About the Advertising?" *Educational Leadership* (December 1993/January 1994): 56–58.

6. For more examples of—and ideas for responding to—this phenomenon, contact the Center for Commercial-Free Public Education (www.commercial free.org) or Commercial Alert (www.commercialalert.org). Also see Alex Molnar, *Giving Kids the Business: The Commercialization of America's Schools* (Boulder, Colo.: Westview, 1996), or contact his Commercialism in Education Research Unit (www.asu.edu/educ/epsl/ceru.htm).

7. "Your child's science teachers may be summering with Weyerhaeuser or the hunting lobby. They may be teaching about our food supply with a lesson plan developed and donated by Monsanto. And the video on how oil is formed? An Exxon production . . . Andrew Hagelshaw, director of the Center for Commercial-Free Public Education in Oakland, said such programs are an attempt to establish brand loyalty. He said the logging companies and oil industry have figured out what fast-food restaurants have long known: 'If you just start educating people at young ages around these facts, then they accept it as truth,' and that means customers for life." See Chris Moran, "Education or Indoctrination?" *San Diego Union-Tribune,* May 13, 2002.

8. David F. Labaree, *How to Succeed in School Without Really Learning: The Credentials Race in American Education* (New Haven, Conn.: Yale University Press, 1997), p. 51.

9. Chubb is quoted in Bernie Froese-Germain, "What We Know About School Choice," *Education Canada* (Fall 1998): 22.

10. Deborah Meier, *The Power of Their Ideas* (Boston: Beacon, 1995), pp. 79, 8, 104, 7.

11. Nick Bromell, "Summa Cum Avaritia," *Harper's* (February 2002): 76.

12. Ethan Bronner, "Better Schools Is Battle Cry for Fall Elections," *New York Times,* September 20, 1998, p. A32.

13. On this point, see Alfie Kohn, "Students Don't 'Work'—They Learn," *Education Week,* September 3, 1997, pp. 60, 43; and Hermine H. Marshall, "Beyond the Workplace Metaphor: The Classroom as a Learning Setting," *Theory Into Practice,* vol. 29, no. 2 (1990): 94–101.

14. Ellwood Cubberley, *Public School Administration* (Boston: Houghton Mifflin, 1916), p. 338.

15. The *Fortune* article is quoted in Daniel Tanner, "Manufacturing Problems and Selling Solutions," *Phi Delta Kappan,* November 2000, p. 198.

16. Linda Darling-Hammond, *The Right to Learn* (San Francisco: Jossey-Bass, 1997), p. 40.

17. Jeff Archer, "New School Role Seen Critical to Respond to Modern Economy," *Education Week,* May 8, 1996, pp. 1, 8; Catherine S. Manegold, "Study Says Schools Must Stress Academics," *New York Times,* September 23, 1994, p. A22; Business Roundtable, *A Business Leader's Guide to Setting Academic Standards* (Washington, D.C.: Business Roundtable, 1996); Mary Ann Zehr, "Manufacturers Endorse National Tests, Vouchers," *Education Week,* January 14, 1998, p. 14; Business Task Force on Student Standards, *The Challenge of Change: Standards to Make Education Work for All Our Children* (Washington, D.C.: National Alliance of Business, 1995).

18. Many writers, of course, have grappled with education's ultimate goals. I attempt to sort through some of the underlying issues in *The Schools Our Children Deserve* (Boston: Houghton Mifflin, 1999), pp. 115–20.

19. See, for example, an analysis of the powerful Business Roundtable, whose "main objective is not quality education but the preservation of the competitiveness of corporate America in the global economy," in Bess Altwerger and Steven L. Strauss, "The Business Behind Testing," *Language Arts,* vol. 79, no. 3 (January 2002): 256–62. Quotation appears on p. 258.

3. The Costs of Overemphasizing Achievement

Only extraordinary education is concerned with learning; most is concerned with achieving: and for young minds, these two are very nearly opposite.

—MARILYN FRENCH

Common sense suggests we should figure out what our educational goals are, then check in periodically to see how successful we have been at meeting them. Assessment thus would be an unobtrusive servant of teaching and learning. Unfortunately, common sense is in short supply today because assessment has come to dominate the whole educational process. Worse, the purposes and design of the most common forms of assessment—both within classrooms and across schools—often lead to disastrous consequences.

Part of the problem is that we shy away from asking the right questions and from following the data where they lead. Instead, we fiddle with relatively trivial details, fine-tuning the techniques of measurement while missing the bigger picture. Take grading, for example. Much of the current discussion focuses on how often to prepare grade reports or what mark should be given for a specified level of achievement (for example, what constitutes "B" work). What we really should be asking is why we are assessing students in the first place.

If we are primarily interested in collecting information that will enhance the quality of learning, then traditional report cards are clearly inferior to more authentic models. Unhappily, assessment is sometimes driven by entirely different objectives—for example, to motivate students (with grades used as carrots and

Originally published in *School Administrator* in 1999.

sticks to coerce them into working harder) or to sort students (the point being not to help everyone learn but to figure out who is better than whom). In either case, the project is doomed from the outset, not because we haven't found the right technique but because there is something fundamentally wrong with our goals.

The practice of sorting children is accomplished not only by grades (the most egregious example being grading on a curve) but also by standardized testing. Not only are the results of so-called norm-referenced tests reported in relative terms (rather than assessing how well each student did according to a fixed standard), but the questions on the tests have been selected with that purpose in mind. The test designers will probably toss out an item that most students manage to answer correctly. Whether it is reasonable for students to know the answer is irrelevant. Thus, to use a test like the ITBS to gauge educational quality, as assessment expert W. James Popham remarked, "is like measuring temperature with a tablespoon."

Standardized tests often have the additional disadvantages of being (a) produced and scored far away from the classroom, (b) multiple choice in design (so students can't generate answers or explain their thinking), (c) timed (so speed matters more than thoughtfulness), and (d) administered on a one-shot, high-anxiety basis.

All of these features represent the very opposite of meaningful assessment. But that doesn't mean these tests are irrelevant to what goes on in classrooms. To the contrary, they have a very powerful impact on instruction, almost always for the worse. Teachers feel increasingly pressured to take time away from real learning in order to prepare students to take these dreadful tests.

Some of this pressure originates from state capitals, of course. However, school district administrators often compound the harm by adding tests, sometimes those that are least informative (by virtue of being norm-referenced) and most destructive (by virtue of how teachers end up creating a dumbed-down, test-driven curriculum). All of this is done, of course, in the name of tougher standards and accountability, but, as any good teacher could tell you, the practical result is that the intellectual life is squeezed out of classrooms.

In fact, researchers could tell you this, too. In a study conducted in Colorado, some fourth-grade teachers were asked to teach a specific task. About half were told that when they were finished, their students must "perform up to standards" and do well on a test. The other teachers, given the identical task, were invited simply to "facilitate the children's learning." At the end, all the students were tested. The result: Students in the standards classrooms did not learn the task as well.

Why? For one thing, when teachers feel pressured to produce results, they tend to pressure their students in turn. That is exactly what was found in a second study, conducted in New York. Teachers became more controlling, removing virtually any opportunity for students to direct their own learning. Since people rarely do their best when they feel controlled, the findings of the Colorado experiment make perfect sense: The more teachers are thinking about test results and "raising the bar," the less well the students actually perform—to say nothing of how their enthusiasm for learning is apt to wane.

A Disturbing Situation

The implications of taking these concerns seriously would be enormous. But even this critique doesn't get to the bottom of what's wrong with the current approach to assessment. The underlying problem concerns a fundamental distinction that has been at the center of some work in educational psychology for a couple of decades now. It is the difference between focusing on *how well* you're doing something and focusing on *what* you're doing.

Consider a school that constantly emphasizes the importance of performance! results! achievement! success! A student who has absorbed that message may find it difficult to get swept away by the process of creating a poem or trying to build a working telescope. He may be so concerned about the results that he's not all that engaged in the activity that produces those results. The two orientations aren't mutually exclusive, of course, but in practice they feel different and lead to different behaviors. Without even knowing how well a student actually did at a task or how smart she is supposed to be, we can tell a lot just from knowing whether she has been led to be more concerned about layers of learning or levels of achievement.

Doesn't it matter how effectively students are learning? Of course it does. It makes sense to sit down with them every so often to figure out how successful they (and we) have been. But when we get carried away with results, we wind up, paradoxically, with results that are less than ideal. Specifically, the evidence suggests that five disturbing consequences are likely to accompany an obsession with standards and achievement:

1. Students come to regard learning as a chore. When kids are encouraged constantly to think about how well they're doing in school, the first casualty is their attitude toward learning. They may come to view the tasks themselves—the stories and science projects and math problems—as material that must be gotten through. It's stuff they're supposed to do better at, not stuff they're excited about exploring. The kind of student who is mostly concerned with being a top performer may persevere at a task, but genuine interest in it or excitement about the whole idea of learning often begins to evaporate as soon as achievement becomes the main point.

This is related to the discovery by psychologists that intrinsic motivation and extrinsic motivation tend to be inversely related: The more people are rewarded for doing something, the more they tend to lose interest in whatever they had to do to get the reward. Thus, it shouldn't be surprising that when students are told they'll need to know something for a test—or, more generally, that something they're about to do will count for a grade—they are likely to find that task (or book or idea) less appealing in its own right.

2. Students try to avoid challenging tasks. If the point is to succeed rather than to stretch one's thinking or discover new ideas, then it is completely logical for a student to want to do whatever is easiest. That, after all, will maximize the probability of success—or at least minimize the probability of failure.

A number of researchers have tested this hypothesis. Typically, in such an experiment, kids are told they're going to be given a task. Some are informed that their performance will be evaluated, while others are encouraged to think of this as an opportunity to learn rather than to do well. Then each student is given a chance to choose how hard a version of the task he or she wants to try. The result is always the same: Those who had been told it's "an opportunity to learn" are more willing to challenge themselves than are those who had been led to think about how well they'll do.

It's convenient for us to assume that kids who cut corners are just being lazy, because then it's the kids who have to be fixed. But perhaps they're just being rational. They have adapted to an environment where results, not intellectual exploration, are what count. When school systems use traditional grading systems—or, worse, when they add honor rolls and other incentives to enhance the significance of grades—they are unwittingly discouraging students from stretching themselves to see what they're capable of doing. It's almost painfully ironic: School officials and reformers complain bitterly about how kids today just want to take the easy way out . . . while simultaneously creating an emphasis on performance and results that leads predictably to that very outcome.

3. Students tend to think less deeply. The goal of some students is to acquire new skills, to find out about the world, to understand what they're doing. When they pick up a book, they're thinking about what they're reading, not about how well they're reading it. Paradoxically, these students who have put success out of their minds are likely to be successful. They process information more deeply, review things they didn't understand the first time, make connections between what they're doing now and what they learned earlier, and use more strategies to make sense of the ideas they're encountering. All of this has been demonstrated empirically.

By contrast, students who have been led to focus on producing the right answer or scoring well on a test tend to think more superficially. Consider just one of dozens of studies on this question, which concerns the ability to transfer understanding—that is, to take something learned over here and apply it to a new task or question over there. As a group of eighth-graders were about to begin a week-long unit in science class, researchers gauged whether each student was more interested in understanding or in being successful. When the unit was over, the students were tested on their ability to transfer their new knowledge. Regardless of whether their earlier test scores had been high or low, the success-oriented students simply did not do as well as those who were more learning-oriented.

4. Students may fall apart when they fail. No one succeeds all the time, and no one can learn very effectively without making mistakes and bumping up against his or her limits. It's important, therefore, to encourage a healthy and resilient attitude toward failure. As a rule, that is exactly what students tend to have if their main goal is to learn: When they do something incorrectly, they see the result as useful information. They figure out what went wrong and how to fix it.

Not so for the kids who believe (often because they have been explicitly told) that the point is to succeed—or even to do better than everyone else. They seem to be fine as long as they are succeeding, but as soon as they hit a bump they may regard themselves as failures and act as though they're helpless to do anything about it. Even a momentary stumble can seem to cancel out all their past successes. When the point isn't to figure things out but to prove how good you are, it's often hard to cope with being less than good.

Consider the student who becomes frantic when he gets a 92 instead of his usual 100. We usually see this as a problem with the individual and conclude that such students are just too hard on themselves. But the "what I'm doing" versus "how well I'm doing" distinction can give us a new lens through which to see what is going on here. It may be the systemic demand for high achievement that led him to become debilitated when he failed, even if the failure is only relative.

The important point isn't what level of performance qualifies as failure (a 92 versus a 40, say). It's the perceived pressure not to fail, which can have a particularly harmful impact on high-achieving and high-ability students. Thus, to reassure such a student that "a 92 is still very good" or that we're sure he'll "do better next time" doesn't just miss the point; it makes things worse by underscoring yet again that the point of school isn't to explore ideas, it's to triumph.

5. Students value ability more than effort. How do we react when a student receives a score of 100 on a quiz? Most teachers and parents treat that as news worth celebrating. Those who are more thoughtful, by contrast, are not necessarily pleased. First of all, they will be concerned about the "bunch o' facts" approach to instruction and assessment that may be reflected by the use of traditional quizzes. Even successful students are not well served by such teaching.

But even when better forms of assessment are used, perceptive observers realize that a student's score is less important than why she thinks she got that score. Let's ask how a student might explain doing especially well on a test. One possibility is *effort:* She tried hard, studied, did all she could to learn the material. A second possibility is *ability:* If you asked her how she got a hundred, she might reply (or think), "Well, I guess I'm just smart." Yet another answer is *luck:* She believes she guessed correctly or was just having a good day. Finally, she might explain the result in terms of the level of *task difficulty*—in this case, the fact that the test was easy. (Notice that these same four reasons could be used by another student to make sense of his grade of 23 on the same quiz: I didn't try hard; I'm just stupid; it was bad luck; or the test was difficult.)

Which of these four explanations for doing well (or poorly) do you favor? Which would you like to see students using to account for their performance in school? Almost everyone would vote for effort. It bodes well for the future when kids attribute a good score to how carefully they prepared for the test. Likewise, those who attribute a low score to not preparing for the test tend to perceive failure as something they can prevent next time. So here's the punch line: When students are led to focus on how well they are performing in school, they tend to explain their performance not by how hard they tried but by how smart they are.

Researchers have demonstrated that a student with a performance focus—How am I doing? Are my grades high enough?

Do I know the right answer?—is likely to interpret these questions "in terms of how much ability [he or she has] and whether or not this ability is adequate to achieve success," as educational psychologist Carol Dweck and a colleague have explained. In their study of academically advanced students, for example, the more that teachers emphasized getting good grades, avoiding mistakes, and keeping up with everyone else, the more the students tended to attribute poor performance to factors they thought were outside their control, such as a lack of ability. When students are made to think constantly about how well they are doing, they are apt to explain the outcome in terms of who they are rather than how hard they tried.

Research also demonstrates that adolescents who explain their achievement in terms of their intelligence tend to think less deeply and carefully about what they're learning than do those who appeal to the idea of effort. Similarly, elementary school students who attribute failure to ability are likely to be poorer readers. And if children are encouraged to think of themselves as "smart" when they succeed, doing poorly on a subsequent task will bring down their achievement even though it doesn't have that effect on other kids.

The upshot of all this is that beliefs about intelligence and about the causes of one's own success and failure matter a lot. They often make more of a difference than how confident students are or what they're truly capable of doing or how they did on last week's exam. If, like the cheerleaders for tougher standards, we look only at the bottom line, only at the test scores and grades, we'll end up overlooking the ways that students make sense of those results. And if we get kids thinking too much about how to improve the bottom line, they may end up making sense of those results in the least constructive way.

Undermining Excellence

If all of this seems radical, it is—in the original, Latin sense of the word *radical*, which means "of the root." Indeed, cutting-edge research raises root questions, including the possibility that the problem with tests is not limited to their content. Rather, the harm comes from paying too much attention to the results. Even the most unbiased, carefully constructed, "authentic" measure of what students know is likely to be worrisome, psychologically speaking, if too big a deal is made about how students did, thus leading them (and their teachers) to think less about learning and more about test outcomes. As Martin Maehr and the late Carol Midgley at the University of Michigan concluded, "An overemphasis on assessment can actually undermine the pursuit of excellence." That's true regardless of the quality of the assessment. Bad tests just multiply the damage.

Most of the time students are in school, particularly younger students but arguably older ones too, they should be able to think and write and explore without worrying about how good they are. Only now and then does it make sense for the teacher to help them attend to how successful they've been and how they can improve. On those occasions, the assessment can and should be done without the use of traditional grades and standardized tests. But most of the time, students should be immersed in learning.

Two: Standards and Testing

4. Confusing Harder with Better

Never underestimate the power of a catchy slogan and a false dichotomy. When a politician pronounces himself a supporter of "law and order" or "a strong defense," you may protest that it's not that simple, but even as you start to explain why, you've already been dismissed as soft on crime or unwilling to defend Our Way of Life.

People who attend to nuance have long been at a disadvantage in politics, where spin is out of control. Never before, however, has the same been quite so true of the public conversation about education, which is distinguished today by simplistic demands for "accountability" and "raising the bar." Not only public officials but business groups and many journalists have played a role in reducing the available options to two: Either you're in favor of higher standards or you are presumably content with lower standards. Choose one.

These days almost anything can be done to students and to schools, no matter how ill-considered, as long as it is done in the name of raising standards. As a result, we are facing a situation in this country that can be described without exaggeration as an educational emergency: Schools are being turned into giant test-prep centers, and many students—as well as some of our finest educators—are being forced out.

Part of the problem is that the enterprise of raising standards in practice means little more than raising the scores on standardized tests, many of which are norm-referenced, multiple-choice, and otherwise flawed. The more schools commit themselves to improving performance on these tests, the more that meaningful opportunities to learn are sacrificed. Thus, high scores are often a sign of *lowered* standards—a paradox rarely appreciated by those who make, or report on, education policy.

Originally published in *Education Week* in 1999.

Compounding the problem is a reliance on the sort of instruction that treats children as passive receptacles into which knowledge or skills are poured. "Back to basics" education—a misnomer, really, because most American schools never left it—might be described as outdated except for the fact that there never was a time when it worked all that well. Modern cognitive science just explains more systematically why this approach has always come up short. When you watch students slogging through textbooks, memorizing lists, being lectured at, and working on isolated skills, you begin to realize that nothing bears a greater responsibility for undermining educational excellence than the continued dominance of traditional instruction. Shrill calls for "accountability" usually just produce an accelerated version of the same thing.

Underlying the kind of pedagogy and assessment associated with the tougher-standards movement is an assumption that has rarely been identified and analyzed—namely, that the main thing wrong with the schools today is that kids get off too easy. Texts and tests and teaching have been "dumbed down," it is alleged. At the heart of metaphors like *raising* standards (or the bar) is the premise that harder is better.

Now, the first and most obvious thing to be said in response is that assignments and exams can be too difficult just as they can be too easy. If the latter can leave students insufficiently challenged, the former can make them feel stupid, which, in turn, can lead them to feel alienated, to lose interest in the subject matter, and sometimes to misbehave. (It's usually less threatening for kids to be seen as incorrigible than as inadequate.) Anyone can ask students questions that are laughably easy *or* impossibly difficult. "The trick," observed Jerome Bruner, "is to find the medium questions that can be answered and that take you somewhere." In short, maximum difficulty isn't the same as optimal difficulty.

But let's delve a little deeper. Maybe the issue isn't whether harder is always better so much as why we focus so much attention on the whole question of difficulty.

John Dewey reminded us that the value of what students do "resides in its connection with a stimulation of greater *thoughtfulness*, not in the greater strain it imposes." If you were making a list of what counts in education—that is, the criteria to use in judging whether students would benefit from what they were doing—the task's difficulty level would be only one factor among many, and almost certainly not the most important. To judge schools by how demanding they are is rather like judging an opera on the basis of how many notes it contains that are hard for singers to hit. In other words, it leaves out most of what matters.

Here's what follows from this recognition: If homework assignments or exams consist of factual-recall questions, it really doesn't make all that much difference whether there are twenty-five tough questions or ten easy ones. Similarly, a textbook does not become a more appropriate teaching tool just because it is intended for a higher grade level. Some parents indignantly complain that their kids are bored and can complete the worksheets without breaking a sweat. They ought to be complaining about the fact that the teacher is relying on worksheets at all. We have to look at the whole method of instruction, the underlying theory of learning, rather than just quibbling about how hard the assignment is or how much the students must strain.

One reason a back-to-basics curriculum fits perfectly with the philosophy of prizing hard work is that it *creates* hard work—often unnecessarily. It's more difficult to learn to read if the task is to decode a string of phonemes than if it is to make sense of interesting stories. It's more exhausting to memorize a list of scientific vocabulary words than it is to learn scientific concepts by devising your own experiment. If kids are going to be forced to learn facts without context, and skills without meaning, it's certainly handy to have an ideology that values difficulty for its own sake. To be sure, learning often requires sustained attention and effort. But there's a vital difference between that which is rigorous and that which is merely onerous.

Other words are similarly slippery. Do we want students to be "challenged" more, or to live up to "higher expectations" in a school that stands for "excellence"? It all depends on how these words are being defined. If they signify a deeper, richer, more engaging curriculum in which students play an active role in integrating ideas and pursuing controversial questions, then you can count on my support. But if these terms are used to justify memorizing more state capitals, or getting a student to bring up her grades (a process that research has shown often undermines the quality of learning), then it's not so clear that rigor and challenge and all the rest of it are worth supporting.

If these distinctions are missed by some parents and teachers, they are systematically ignored by the purveyors of tougher standards. Recently, my own state introduced a test that students must pass in order to receive a high school diploma. It requires them to acquire a staggering number of facts, which allowed policymakers to claim proudly that they had raised the bar. After new proficiency exams were failed by a significant proportion of students in several other states, education officials there responded by making the tests even harder the following year. The commissioner of education for Colorado offered some insight into the sensibility underlying such decisions: "Unless you get bad results," he declared, "it is highly doubtful you have done anything useful with your tests. Low scores have become synonymous with good tests." Such is the logic on which the tougher-standards movement has been built.

But how many adults could pass these exams? How many high school teachers possess the requisite stock of information outside their own subjects? How many college professors, for that matter, or business executives, or state legislators could confidently write an essay about Mayan agricultural practices or divergent plate boundaries? We would do well to adopt (Deborah) Meier's Mandate: *No student should be expected to meet an academic requirement that a cross section of successful adults in the community cannot.*

(In the same spirit, I propose Kohn's Corollary to Meier's Mandate: All persons given to pious rhetoric about the need to "raise standards" and produce "world-class academic performance for the twenty-first century" not only should be required to take these exams themselves but must agree to have their scores published in the newspaper.)

Beyond the issue of how many of us could meet these standards is an equally provocative question: How many of us *need* to know this stuff—not just on the basis of job requirements but as a reflection of what it means to be well educated? Do these facts and skills reflect what we honor, what matters to us about schooling and human life? Often, the standards being rammed into our children's classrooms are not merely unreasonable but irrelevant. It is the kinds of things students are being forced to learn, and the approach to learning itself, that don't ring true. The tests that result—for students and sometimes for teachers—are not just ridiculously difficult but simply ridiculous.

"It is not enough to be busy," Henry David Thoreau once remarked. "The question is, what are we busy about?" If our students are memorizing more forgettable facts than ever before, if they are spending their hours being drilled on what will help them ace a standardized test, then we may indeed have raised the bar—and more's the pity. In that case, school may be harder, but it sure as hell isn't any better.

5. Beware of the Standards, Not Just the Tests

A number of prominent educators are finally raising their voices against standardized testing—particularly multiple-choice, norm-referenced tests; particularly tests with "high stakes" (read: bribes and threats) attached; and particularly in the context of a federal mandate to force every state to test every student in grades three through eight every year. Yet even as more opinion leaders come to understand the damage attributable to testing mania, it is still rare to hear objections to the standards movement as a whole.

The Learning First Alliance, a coalition of leading education groups, cautiously raised concerns about the tests not long ago, but mostly out of fear that the burgeoning grassroots opposition might bring down the state standards, too. *Education Week*'s 2001 edition of *Quality Counts* likewise worried that tests "are overshadowing" and "do not adequately reflect" the standards. Major conferences carry titles such as "Standards: From Theory to Practice" and "Will Standards Survive the Classroom?" (You will look in vain for conferences called "Will Classrooms Survive the Standards?" or "Standards: From Capitulation to Resistance.")

A list of boat-rocking books on the subject begins and pretty much ends with Susan Ohanian's *One Size Fits Few* and Deborah Meier's *Will Standards Save Public Education?* Alarms have been quietly raised by Nel Noddings, Elliot Eisner, James Beane, and a few other eminent educators in the pages of *Phi Delta Kappan*. Otherwise, the field seems to have closed ranks around the idea that it is permissible to criticize the tests, but not the standards. Indeed, test opponents are sternly reminded to avoid confusing the two, as though they were in fact unrelated. I want to argue not

Originally published in *Education Week* in 2001.

only that they are inextricably connected—the tests serving, at least in theory, as the enforcement mechanism of the standards—but also that the latter may be every bit as problematic as the former.

Of course, it's reasonable to ask just what kind of standards are at issue here. The most relevant and widely accepted distinction is between outcome and content. Outcome standards specify how well students must do. At the highest level of generality ("We support high standards"), the notion is unobjectionable but not terribly useful. When translated into specifics, it comes to mean cut scores on standardized tests and becomes downright dangerous. Outcome standards to a remarkable extent are based on confusing harder with better, an error I discussed in the previous chapter.

Content standards, by contrast, specify what students will be taught. Rather than declaring that all such standards are bad —or, as is far more common, accepting all such standards uncritically—I propose that we judge a given set of standards or frameworks according to four criteria:

How specific? There are many reasons policymakers seek to impose detailed curriculum mandates. They may fundamentally distrust educators: Much of the current standards movement is just the latest episode in a long, sorry history of trying to create a teacher-proof curriculum. Alternatively, they may simply assume that more specificity is always preferable. In reality, just because it makes sense to explain to a waiter exactly how I'd like my burger cooked doesn't mean it's better to declare that students will study the perimeter of polygons (along with scores of other particular topics) than it is to offer broad guidelines for helping students learn to think like mathematicians.

The latter sort of standards, supported by practical guidance, can help students reason carefully, communicate clearly, and get a kick out of doing so. But long lists of facts and skills that teachers must cover may have the opposite effect. Thus, when the late Harold Howe II, the U.S. commissioner of education under President Lyndon Johnson, was asked what a set of national standards should be like (if we had to adopt them), he summarized a lifetime of wisdom in four words: "as vague as possible."

His caution applies to state standards as well. On the one hand, thinking is messy, and deep thinking is very messy. On the other hand, standards documents are nothing if not orderly. Keep that contrast in mind and you will not be surprised to see how much damage those documents can do in real classrooms.

Considerable research has demonstrated the importance of making sure students are actively involved in designing their own learning, invited to play a role in formulating questions, creating projects, and so on. But the more comprehensive and detailed a list of standards, the more students (and even teachers) are excluded from this process, the more alienated they tend to become, and the more teaching becomes a race to cover a huge amount of material. Thus, meeting these kinds of standards may actually have the effect of dumbing down classrooms. As Howard Gardner and his colleagues wisely observed, "The greatest enemy of understanding is 'coverage.'"

Some insist that these lists of facts and skills don't prescribe how students will be taught; the standards are said to be neutral with respect to pedagogy. But this is nonsense. If the goal is to cover material (rather than, say, to discover ideas), that unavoidably informs the methods that will be used. Techniques such as repetitive drill-and-practice are privileged by curriculum frameworks based on a "bunch o' facts" approach to education. Of course, that kind of teaching is also driven by an imperative to prepare students for tests, but no less by an imperative to conform to specific standards.

How quantifiable? The current accountability fad insists on mandates that are not only overly detailed but chosen according to whether they lend themselves to easy measurement. It's not just that the tests are supposed to be tied to the standards; it's that the standards have been selected on the basis of their testability. The phrase *specific, measurable standards* suggests a commitment not to excellence but to behaviorism. It is telling that this phrase is heard most often from corporate officials and politicians, not from leading educational theorists or cognitive scientists.

We are talking about a worldview in which any aspect of learning, or life, that resists being reduced to numbers is regarded as vaguely suspicious. By contrast, anything that appears in numerical form seems reassuringly scientific; if the numbers are getting larger over time, we must be making progress. Concepts like intrinsic motivation and intellectual exploration are difficult for some minds to grasp, whereas test scores, like sales figures or votes, can be calculated and charted and used to define success and failure.

Unfortunately, meaningful learning does not always proceed along a single dimension, such that we can nail down the extent of improvement. As Linda McNeil of Rice University has observed, "Measurable outcomes may be the least significant results of learning." (That sentence ought to be printed out in 36-point Helvetica, framed, and hung on the wall of every school administrator's office in the country.) To talk about what happens in schools as moving forward or backward in specifiable degrees is not only simplistic, in the sense that it fails to capture what is actually going on; it is destructive, because it can change what is going on for the worse.

Consider a comment made by Sandra Stotsky, the deputy commissioner of education in Massachusetts: "*Explore* isn't a word that can be put into a standard because it can't be assessed."

This assertion is obviously false, because there are plenty of ways to assess the quality of students' exploration—unless, of course, "assessment" is equated with standardized testing. But suppose for the moment that Ms. Stotsky was correct. What if we really were faced with a trade-off between an emphasis on exploration in the classroom and the demands of measurement? Most thoughtful educators would unhesitatingly choose the former, whereas those who write and enforce state standards often opt for the latter. Clearly, it is much easier to quantify the number of times a semicolon has been used correctly in an essay than it is to quantify how well the student has explored ideas in that essay. Thus, the more emphasis that is placed on picking standards that are measurable, the less ambitious the teaching will become.

How uniform? We have heard the phrase *standardized testing* so often that we may have become inured to the significance of that first word. To what extent do we really want our students to receive a standardized education? At a national conference in fall 2000, a consultant announced with apparent satisfaction that now, thanks to standards-based reform, "for the first time in my experience, people on a grade level, in a subject area, or teaching a course at a high school are [feeling] a responsibility to all have the same destination." That she did not even feel it necessary to defend this goal says something about the current acceptance of a one-size-fits-all model of education.

Once again, the problem is not just with the construction of the tests, but with the uniformity of the standards. Wanting to make sure that students in low-income communities don't receive a second-rate education is a laudable objective. Wanting to make sure that all students in your state receive the *same* education is a very different matter. Even more troubling are grade-by-grade standards. Here, the prescribers are not just saying, "We expect students to know the following stuff by the time they're in eighth grade," but "We expect them to learn all the items on this list in fifth grade, all the items on that list in sixth grade," and so on. Apart from the negative effects on learning, this rigidity about both the timing of the instruction and its content creates failures unnecessarily by trying to force all children to learn at the same pace.

Guidelines or mandates? There are standards offered as guidelines ("See if this way of thinking about teaching can help you improve your craft"), and then there are standards presented as mandates ("Teach this or else"). Virtually all the states have chosen the latter course. The effect has been not only to control teachers, but to usurp the long-established power of local school districts to chart their own course. If there has ever been a more profoundly undemocratic school reform movement in U.S. educational history than what is currently taking place in the name of standards, I haven't heard of it.

Bullying reaches its apotheosis with high-stakes testing, the use of crude rewards and punishments to make people ratchet up the scores. The underlying logic is captured by an ironic sign spotted on a classroom wall: "The beatings will continue until morale improves." But the standards themselves, if handed down as requirements, embody that same determination on the part of policymakers to do things *to* educators and students rather than to work *with* them. My nominee for the most chillingly Orwellian word now in widespread use is "alignment"—as in, "How can we make teachers 'align' their teaching to the state standards?" A remarkable number of people, including some critics of high-stakes testing, have casually accepted this sort of talk despite the fact that it is an appeal to naked power. "Alignment" isn't about improvement; it's about conformity.

Standards-as-mandates also imply a rather insulting view of educators—namely, that they need to be told what (and, by extension, how) to teach by someone in authority because otherwise they wouldn't know. While plenty of teachers need help, virtually everyone is likely to resist having the state try to micromanage his or her classroom. Some will do their best to ignore the standards, while others will comply resentfully. Either way, the use of control leads to poor implementation of the standards (which, come to think of it, may not be such a bad thing). Others, including some of our best educators, will throw up their hands in disgust and find another career.

Based on these four criteria, the standards promulgated by disciplinary groups (the councils of teachers of mathematics and English, for example) come out considerably better than the standards issued by states. This doesn't preclude our objecting to certain aspects of the former documents, of course, nor does it mean that all state standards are equally bad.

Currently, however, there is considerable pressure to implement the kind of standards that I am suggesting are the worst. Chester E. Finn Jr. and his colleagues want states to spell out "which books children should read in English class, which individuals and events to study in history, and so on"; any other standards are simply "fluff." Pro-standards groups such as Achieve Inc. (a group of corporate officials and politicians) tend to give poor ratings to states whose standards aren't sufficiently specific, measurable, uniform, or compulsory.

The difference between these evaluations and a report by, say, the National Rifle Association that assigns low grades to legislators who are not sufficiently pro-gun is that in the latter case everyone realizes the ratings reflect a specific and very debatable point of view. By contrast, those who mark down a state for granting too much autonomy to local school boards, or for having standards that wouldn't satisfy behaviorists, would like us to accept this as an objective evaluation. (One could make a case that states given an A in annual evaluations really deserve an F, and vice versa—or that a state should commission a review of its standards and testing policy by one of these groups and then do precisely the opposite of what is recommended.)

An important side note here: There has been some grumbling lately about the use of off-the-shelf tests that are unrelated to the state's standards documents—for example, in California. From a psychometric perspective, this practice doesn't make much sense. From a pedagogical perspective, though, the only thing worse than tests that aren't aligned to the standards are tests that *are* aligned to the standards. The former is silly because it is inefficient, while the latter is dangerous precisely because it is efficient . . . at accomplishing a dubious goal. Not only politicians but also some assessment experts sometimes forget that doing something well is not the same as doing something that's worthwhile. When the standards and tests fit together perfectly to create an airtight system of top-down, uniform, fact-oriented schooling—well, that's when we're really in trouble.

The tests arguably constitute the most serious and immediate threat to good teaching, such that freeing educators and students from their yoke should be our top priority. But we should not limit our critique to the testing, which is, after all, one manifestation of a larger, and seriously wrong-headed, approach to pedagogy and school reform.

I am not troubled by those who disagree with my criteria or who like a given set of standards more than I do. In fact, I welcome such challenges. What troubles me is the rarity of such discussion, the absence of questioning, the tendency to offer instruction about how to teach to the standards before we have even asked whether doing so is a sound idea.

6. Standardized Testing and Its Victims

Standardized testing has swelled and mutated, like a creature in one of those old horror movies, to the point that it now threatens to swallow our schools whole. (Of course, on "The Late, Late Show," no one ever insists that the monster is really doing us a favor by making its victims more "accountable.") But let's put aside metaphors and even opinions for a moment so that we can review some indisputable facts on the subject.

Fact 1. *Our children are tested to an extent that is unprecedented in our history and unparalleled anywhere else in the world.* While previous generations of American students have had to sit through tests, never have the tests been given so frequently, and never have they played such a prominent role in schooling. The current situation is also unusual from an international perspective: Few countries use standardized tests for children below high school age—or multiple-choice tests for students of any age.

Fact 2. *Noninstructional factors explain most of the variance among test scores when schools or districts are compared.* A study of math results on the 1992 National Assessment of Educational Progress found that the combination of four such variables (number of parents living at home, parents' educational background, type of community, and poverty rate) accounted for a whopping 89 percent of the differences in state scores. To the best of my knowledge, all such analyses of state tests have found comparable results, with the numbers varying only slightly as a function of which socioeconomic variables were considered.

Fact 3. *Norm-referenced tests were never intended to measure the quality of learning or teaching.* The Stanford, Metropolitan, and California Achievement Tests (SAT, MAT, and CAT), as well

Originally published in *Education Week* in 2000.

as the Iowa and Comprehensive Tests of Basic Skills (ITBS and CTBS), are designed so that only about half the test-takers will respond correctly to most items. The main objective of these tests is to rank, not to rate; to spread out the scores, not to gauge the quality of a given student or school.

Fact 4. *Standardized-test scores often measure superficial thinking.* In a study published in the *Journal of Educational Psychology*, elementary school students were classified as "actively" engaged in learning if they asked questions of themselves while they read and tried to connect what they were doing to past learning; and as "superficially" engaged if they just copied down answers, guessed a lot, and skipped the hard parts. It turned out that high scores on both the CTBS and the MAT were more likely to be found among students who exhibited the superficial approach to learning. Similar findings have emerged from studies of middle school students (also using the CTBS) and high school students (using the other SAT, the college-admission exam). To be sure, there are plenty of students who think deeply *and* score well on tests—and plenty of students who do neither. But, as a rule, it appears that standardized-test results are positively correlated with a shallow approach to learning.

Fact 5. *Virtually all specialists condemn the practice of giving standardized tests to children younger than eight or nine years old.* I say "virtually" to cover myself here, but, in fact, I have yet to find a single reputable scholar in the field of early-childhood education who endorses such testing for young children.

Fact 6. *Virtually all relevant experts and organizations condemn the practice of basing important decisions, such as graduation or promotion, on the results of a single test.* The National Research Council takes this position, as do most other professional groups (such as the American Educational Research Association and the American Psychological Association), the generally pro-testing

American Federation of Teachers, and even the companies that manufacture and sell the exams. Yet just such high-stakes testing is currently taking place, or scheduled to be introduced soon, in more than half the states.

Fact 7. *The time, energy, and money that are being devoted to preparing students for standardized tests have to come from somewhere.* (For more, see the following chapter.)

Fact 8. *Many educators are leaving the field because of what is being done to schools in the name of "accountability" and "tougher standards."* I have no hard numbers here, but there is more than enough anecdotal evidence—corroborated by administrators, teacher-educators, and other observers across the country, and supported by several state surveys that quantify the extent of disenchantment with testing—to warrant classifying this as a fact. Prospective teachers are rethinking whether they want to begin a career in which high test scores matter most, and in which they will be pressured to produce these scores. Similarly, as the *New York Times* reported in its lead story of September 3, 2000, "a growing number of schools are rudderless, struggling to replace a graying corps of principals at a time when the pressure to raise test scores and other new demands have made an already difficult job an increasingly thankless one." It also seems clear that most of the people who are quitting, or seriously thinking about doing so, are not mediocre performers who are afraid of being held accountable. Rather, they are among the very best educators, frustrated by the difficulty of doing high-quality teaching in the current climate.

Faced with inconvenient facts such as these, the leading fallback position for defenders of standardized testing runs as follows: Even if it's true that suburban schools are being dumbed down by the tests, inner-city schools are often horrendous to begin with. There, at least, standards are finally being raised as a result of high-stakes testing.

Let's assume this argument is made in good faith, rather than as a cover for pursuing a standards-and-testing agenda for other reasons. Moreover, let's immediately concede the major premise here, that low-income minority students have been badly served for years. The problem is that the cure is in many ways worse than the disease—and not only because of the preceding eight facts, which remain both stubbornly true and painfully relevant to testing in the inner city. As the late Senator Paul Wellstone, D-Minn., put it in a speech in 2000: "Making students accountable for test scores works well on a bumper sticker, and it allows many politicians to look good by saying that they will not tolerate failure. But it represents a hollow promise. Far from improving education, high-stakes testing marks a major retreat from fairness, from accuracy, from quality, and from equity." Here's why.

The tests may be biased. For decades, critics have complained that many standardized tests are unfair because the questions require a set of knowledge and skills more likely to be possessed by children from a privileged background. The discriminatory effect is particularly pronounced with norm-referenced tests, where the imperative to spread out the scores often produces questions that tap knowledge gained outside of school. This, as W. James Popham argues, provides a powerful advantage to students whose parents are affluent and well educated. It's more than a little ironic to rely on biased tests to "close the gap" between rich and poor.

Guess who can afford better test preparation? When the stakes rise, people seek help anywhere they can find it, and companies eager to profit from this desperation by selling test-prep materials and services have begun to appear on the scene, most recently tailoring their products to state exams. Naturally, affluent families, schools, and districts are better able to afford such products, and the most effective versions of such products, thereby exacerbating the inequity of such testing. Moreover, when poorer schools do manage to scrape together the money to buy these materials, it's often at the expense of books and other educational resources that they really need.

The quality of instruction declines most for those who have least. Standardized tests tend to measure the temporary acquisition of facts and skills, including the skill of test-taking itself, more than genuine understanding. To that extent, the fact that such tests are more likely to be used and emphasized in schools with higher percentages of minority students (a fact that has been empirically verified) predictably results in poorer-quality teaching in such schools. The use of a high-stakes strategy only underscores the preoccupation with these tests and, as a result, accelerates a reliance on direct-instruction techniques and endless practice tests. "Skills-based instruction, the type to which most children of color are subjected, tends to foster low-level uniformity and subvert academic potential," as Dorothy Strickland, an African-American professor at Rutgers University, has remarked.

Again, there's no denying that many schools serving low-income children of color were second-rate to begin with. Now, however, some of these schools, in Chicago, Houston, Baltimore, and elsewhere, are arguably becoming third-rate as testing pressures lead to a more systematic use of low-level, drill-and-skill teaching, often in the context of packaged programs purchased by school districts. Thus, when someone emphasizes the importance of "higher expectations" for minority children, we might reply, "Higher expectations to do what? Bubble-in more ovals correctly on a bad test—or pursue engaging projects that promote sophisticated thinking?" The movement driven by "tougher standards," "accountability," and similar slogans arguably lowers meaningful expectations insofar as it relies on standardized testing as the primary measure of achievement. The more that poor children fill in worksheets on command (in an effort to raise their test scores), the further they fall behind affluent kids who are more likely to get lessons that help them understand ideas. If the drilling does result in higher scores, the proper response is not celebration, but outrage: The test results may well have improved at the expense of real learning.

Standards aren't the main ingredient that's in low supply. Anyone who is serious about addressing the inequities of American education would naturally want to investigate differences in available resources. A good argument could be made that the fairest allocation strategy, which is only common sense in some countries, is to provide not merely equal amounts across schools and districts, but more for the most challenging student populations. This does happen in some states—by no means all—but, even when it does, the money is commonly offered as a short-term grant (hardly sufficient to compensate for years of inadequate funding) and is often earmarked for test preparation rather than for higher-quality teaching. Worse, high-stakes testing systems may provide more money to those already successful (for example, in the form of bonuses for good scores) and less to those whose need is greatest.

Many public officials, along with like-minded journalists and other observers, are apt to minimize the matter of resources and assume that everything deficient about education for poor and minority children can be remedied by more forceful demands that we "raise the bar." The implication here would seem to be that teachers and students could be doing a better job but have, for some reason, chosen not to do so and need only be bribed or threatened into improvement. The focus among policymakers has been on standards of outcome rather than standards of opportunity.

To make matters worse, some supporters of high-stakes testing have not just ignored, but contemptuously dismissed, the relevance of barriers to achievement in certain neighborhoods. Explanations about very real obstacles such as racism, poverty, fear of crime, low teacher salaries, inadequate facilities, and language barriers are sometimes written off as mere "excuses." This is at once naive and callous, and, like any other example of minimizing the relevance of structural constraints, ultimately serves the interests of those fortunate enough not to face them.

Those allegedly being helped will be driven out. When rewards and punishments are applied to educators, those who teach low-scoring populations are the most likely to be branded as failures and may decide to leave the profession. Minority and low-income students are disproportionately affected by the incessant pressure on teachers to raise scores. But when high stakes are applied to the students themselves, there is little doubt about who is most likely to be denied diplomas as a consequence of failing an exit exam—or who will simply give up and drop out in anticipation of such an outcome. If states persist in making a student's fate rest on a single test, the likely result over the next few years will be nothing short of catastrophic. Unless we act to stop this, we will be facing a scenario that might be described without exaggeration as an educational ethnic cleansing.

Let's be charitable and assume that the ethnic aspect of this perfectly predictable consequence is unintentional. Still, it is hard to deny that high-stakes testing, even when the tests aren't norm-referenced, is ultimately about sorting. Someone unfamiliar with the relevant psychological research (and with reality) might insist that raising the bar will "motivate" more students to succeed. But perform the following thought experiment: Imagine that almost all the students in a given state met the standards and passed the tests. What would be the reaction from most politicians, businesspeople, and pundits? Would they now concede that our public schools are terrific—or would they take this result as prima facie evidence that the standards were too low and the tests were too easy? As Deborah Meier and others have observed, the phrase *high standards* by definition means standards that everyone won't be able to meet.

The tests are just the means by which this game is played. It is a game that a lot of kids—predominantly kids of color —simply cannot win. Invoking these very kids to justify a top-down, heavy-handed, corporate-style, test-driven version of school reform requires a stunning degree of audacity. To take the cause of equity seriously is to work for the elimination of tracking, for more equitable funding, and for the universal implementation of more sophisticated approaches to pedagogy (as opposed to heavily scripted direct-instruction programs). But standardized testing, while bad news across the board, is especially hurtful to the students who need our help the most.

7. Sacrificing Learning for Higher Scores

Heated debate continues about whether standardized exams are accurate indicators of children's capabilities and whether students ought to be flunked or prevented from graduating on the basis of a single score. Less attention has been paid to an equally important question: Given that time and energy are limited, what is being sacrificed when schools are forced to focus on test results?

The answers are increasingly clear—and disturbing—as evidence accumulates from across the United States:

• Science and social studies have been severely trimmed in states that do not include those subjects on standardized tests. For example, according to two Texas researchers, Linda McNeil at Rice University and Angela Valenzuela at the University of Texas, "Many science teachers in schools with poor and minority children are required by their principals to suspend the teaching of science for weeks, and in some cases for months, in order to devote science class time to drill and practice" on the Texas test. (Higher test scores are then widely cited as evidence of school improvement.)

• Despite the nearly unanimous view of experts that play is critical to development, recess has been cut back as a result of testing pressures. In Atlanta, where recess was simply eliminated, at least one new school was built without a playground. A survey of 225 Massachusetts school districts found that many schools have cut physical education programs in half, with some offering only thirty minutes per week. Parents in Virginia Beach and Palm Beach County, Florida, have resorted to petition drives to bring back recess.

Originally published in *USA Today* in 2001.

- "The arts and music have all but disappeared from many schools" in Washington, reports the *Seattle Times,* a vanishing act observed from coast to coast.

- Because most tests focus on isolated language skills—or, at best, analysis of short fragments of text—many children are finding less opportunity to read real books. One New York City teacher, compelled to use a heavily scripted program called "Success for All," was asked whether she was still allowing her students to read books of their own choosing. She replied: "We haven't been doing *any* reading since we started preparing the kids for the reading test."

- Community service, character education, democratic class meetings, and other programs to help children become good people as well as good learners have been sharply reduced. One primary-grade teacher in Milwaukee told that city's school board in June 2001 that frequent testing of her students means they can no longer contribute to a Thanksgiving dinner for homeless people or prepare games for cancer patients at a children's hospital.

- Extended activities in which students solve complicated problems, apply skills to real-life situations, or design projects covering many subject areas are increasingly in short supply. Among the lessons eliminated in the name of "raising standards": a Boston school's in-depth unit in which each class studied one country, culminating in a schoolwide international fair; and a medical mentorship program that paired New Rochelle, New York, teens with doctors.

- There are fewer opportunities to learn outside the classroom. All field trips in Ravenswood City, California, elementary schools were suspended until after the spring testing cycle.

The list goes on. From high-quality high school electives to focused discussions of current events, some of the richest learning opportunities are being squeezed out. And all this was before the enactment of a new federal requirement for even more testing.

For policy makers, it may seem reasonable to demand "tougher standards" and to recite slogans such as "accountability." But in real schools, things look quite different. We need to think carefully about the trade-offs the current school-reform movement entails. Indeed, the evidence suggests that higher scores in a given school or community may actually be cause for concern. Reports of rising test performance should lead us to ask, "What was taken away from my children's education in order to make them better at taking standardized tests?"

8. Two Cheers for an End to the SAT

One imagines the folks at the College Board blushing deeply when, a few years back, they announced that the *A* in SAT no longer stood for "Aptitude." Scarlet, after all, would be an appropriate color to turn while, in effect, conceding that the test wasn't—and, let's face it, never had been—a measure of intellectual aptitude. For a brief period, the examination was rechristened the Scholastic Assessment Test, a name presumably generated by the Department of Redundancy Department. Today, literally—and perhaps figuratively—SAT doesn't stand for anything at all.

It wasn't the significance of the shift in the SAT's name that recently produced an epiphany for Richard C. Atkinson, president of the University of California. Rather, the tipping point in his decision to urge the elimination of the SAT as a requirement for admission came last year during a visit to the upscale private school his grandchildren attend. There, he watched as twelve-year-olds were drilled on verbal analogies, part of an extended training that, he said in announcing his proposal, "was not aimed at developing the students' reading and writing abilities but rather their test-taking skills." More broadly, he argued, "America's overemphasis on the SAT is compromising our educational system."

Of course, it must be pointed out that UC, assuming its policymaking bodies accept their president's advice, would not be the first institution to drop the SAT. Hundreds of colleges and universities, including Bates, Bowdoin, Connecticut, and Mount Holyoke Colleges, no longer require the SAT or ACT. A survey by FairTest, an advocacy group based in Cambridge, Massachusetts, reported that such colleges are generally well satisfied that "ap-

Originally published in the *Chronicle of Higher Education* in 2001.

plicant pools and enrolled classes have become more diverse without any loss in academic quality."

On balance, this latest and most significant challenge to the reign of the SAT is very welcome news indeed. There is a possible downside as well, but we should begin by recognizing that even before colleges began hopping off the SAT bandwagon, the assumption that they needed something like the test to help them decide whom to admit was difficult to defend, if only because of a powerful counterexample to our north: No such test is used in Canada. But the more one learns about the SAT in particular, the more one wonders what took Atkinson so long, and what is taking many of his counterparts even longer. Consider:

The SAT is a measure of resources more than of reasoning. Year after year, the College Board's own statistics depict a virtually linear correlation between SAT scores and family income. Each rise in earnings (measured in $10,000 increments) brings a commensurate rise in scores. Other research, meanwhile, has found that more than half the difference among students' scores can be explained purely on the basis of parents' level of education.

Aggregate scores don't reflect educational achievement. SAT results are still sometimes used to compare one state with another or one year with another. Unfortunately, not only is the test voluntary, but participation rates vary enormously by state and district. Brian Powell and Lala Carr Steelman, writing in a 1996 issue of the *Harvard Educational Review,* reported that those rates account for a whopping 85 percent of the variance in scores; when fewer students take the test, a state's results end up looking much better. Similarly, even if it is true that average national scores have declined over the decades (once we factor in the statistical readjustment that took place in 1996), that is mostly because more students, relatively speaking, are now taking the test.

Individual scores don't reflect a student's intellectual depth. The verbal section of the SAT is basically just a vocabulary test. It is not a measure of aptitude or of subject-area competency. So what does it measure, other than the size of students' houses?

An interesting 1995 study with students at East Carolina University classified them as taking a "surface" approach to their assignments (meaning they memorized facts and did as little as possible); a "deep" approach (informed by a genuine desire to understand and a penchant for connecting current lessons with previous knowledge); or an "achieving" approach (where performance, particularly as compared with that of others, mattered more than learning). SAT scores turned out to be significantly correlated with both the surface and achieving approaches, but not at all with the deep approach. That finding has been replicated with the results of other standardized tests taken by younger students, lending support to the criticism that such examinations tend to measure what matters least. (See page 55.)

SAT's don't predict the future. A considerable amount of research, including but not limited to a summary of more than six hundred studies published by the College Board in 1984, has found that only about 12 to 16 percent of the variance in freshman grades could be explained by SAT scores, suggesting that they are not particularly useful even with respect to that limited variable—and virtually worthless at predicting how students will fare after their freshman year (and whether they will graduate).

SAT's don't contribute to diversity. Far from offering talented minority students a way to prove their worth, the overall effect of the SAT has been to ratify entrenched patterns of discrimination. Maria Blanco, a regional counsel with the Mexican American Legal Defense and Educational Fund, remarked recently that the SAT "has turned into a barrier to students of color," because it "keeps out very qualified kids who have overcome obstacles but don't test very well." Colleges looking to put together a racially and ethnically diverse student body are, therefore, already likely to minimize the significance of standardized-test scores.

Unhappily, though, some people committed to affirmative action—and even more who are opposed to it—have treated the SAT as a marker for merit and then argued about whether it is legitimate to set scores aside. Should a desire for equity sometimes override the desire for excellence? But that question is utterly misconceived. SAT's, like other standardized tests, do not further the cause of equity *or* excellence. Such tests privilege the privileged and reflect a skill at taking tests. Few people—other than those who profit handsomely from its administration—will mourn the SAT when it finally breathes its last.

And now the bad news: Unless we are very careful, a long-overdue move to jettison SAT scores may simply ratchet up the significance accorded to other admissions criteria that are little better and possibly even worse. Atkinson suggested that, at least in the short run, colleges might switch to the SAT II, better known as achievement tests. (Subsequently, the College Board announced plans to revamp the SAT I to make its verbal section more similar to some of those same achievement tests.) While that could be considered a step forward in some respects, it may have the effect of creating a standardized, exam-based high school curriculum that squeezes out other kinds of teaching. That is already beginning to happen as states impose their own exit tests: Teachers feel compelled to cover vast amounts of content, often superficially, rather than letting students *dis*cover ideas.

The more ominous threat, though, is that, as the SAT fades, it will be replaced by high school grades. There is a widespread assumption that less emphasis on scores as an admissions criterion has to mean more emphasis on grades, as though nature has decreed an inverse relationship between the two. But for grades to be given more emphasis would be terribly unfortunate. On the most obvious level, grades are unreliable indicators of student achievement. But what is far more disturbing about even the current emphasis on grades, let alone the prospect of enhancing their significance, is the damage they do when students are led to compulsively groom their transcripts. (See chapter 9.) If it's worrisome that SAT coaching sessions take time away from meaningful intellectual pursuits, then it's worse that an admissions policy that causes students to become obsessed with grades could undermine the intellectual value of virtually everything they do in high school. Indeed, it can create intellectual dispositions that persist in and beyond college.

The only thing worse than placing added emphasis on the GPA is placing added emphasis on *relative* GPA. Some state systems now want to guarantee acceptance to all students in a top percentage of their class. Here, the emphasis is not merely on performance (as opposed to learning), but on victory. A considerable body of data demonstrates that creating competition among students is decidedly detrimental with respect to achievement and motivation to learn. The urgent question should not be whether high school class rank is correlated with college grades, but whether secondary schools can maintain (or create) a focus on intellectual exploration when their students are forced to view their classmates as rivals.

Where does all this leave us? Those willing to ask the truly radical questions about college admissions might consider an observation offered thirty years ago during a public lecture at the Educational Testing Service by the psychologist David McClelland. Rather than asking what criteria best predict success in higher education, he asked whether colleges should even be looking for the most-qualified students. "One would think that the purpose of education is precisely to improve the performance of those who are not doing very well," he mused. "If the colleges were interested in proving that they could educate people, high-scoring students might be poor bets because they would be less likely to show improvement in performance."

Many of us will find that challenge too unsettling, preferring that we continue to admit those students who will probably be easiest to educate. But even if we are looking for the "best" students, we ought to see GPA numbers and SAT scores as a matched set of flawed criteria. Grades and tests, at best, will predict future grades and tests. There is good evidence that grades don't predict later-life success, in occupational or intellectual terms. In the 1980s, a review of thirty-five studies, published in the *American Educational Research Journal,* concluded that academic indicators (grades and tests) from college—never mind high school—accounted for less than 3 percent of the variance in eventual occupational performance as judged by income, job-effectiveness ratings, and job satisfaction. Moreover, those indicators had no predictive power whatsoever for M.D.'s and Ph.D.'s.

When Mount Holyoke College, after a lengthy study by faculty members, announced in 2000 that it would stop requiring students to submit SAT scores, the president, Joanne Creighton, did not limit her criticism to that test. "There has been a kind of reductionism in higher education, reducing students and institutions to numbers," she said. Similarly, Atkinson in California said that he had recommended "that all campuses move away from admission processes that use narrowly defined quantitative formulas and instead adopt procedures that look at applicants in a comprehensive, holistic way."

Doing so will not be an easy sell, if only because it is faster and therefore cheaper for universities that hear from tens of thousands of applicants to continue reducing each one to a numerical formula, rather than to weigh each as an individual. A move from SAT to GPA—or SAT I to SAT II—will merely fine-tune the formula. That would be a pity, because the attention given Atkinson's proposal has provided us with an opportunity to confront larger and more lasting issues.

Three: Grading and Evaluating

9. From Degrading to De-Grading

You can tell a lot about a teacher's values and personality just by asking how he or she feels about giving grades. Some defend the practice, claiming that grades are necessary to "motivate" students. Many of these teachers actually seem to enjoy keeping intricate records of students' marks. Such teachers periodically warn students that they're "going to have to know this for the test" as a way of compelling them to pay attention or do the assigned readings—and they may even use surprise quizzes for that purpose, keeping their grade books at the ready.

Frankly, we ought to be worried for these teachers' students. In my experience, the most impressive teachers are those who despise the whole process of giving grades. Their aversion, as it turns out, is supported by solid evidence that raises questions about the very idea of traditional grading.

Three Main Effects of Grading

Researchers have found three consistent effects of using— and especially, emphasizing the importance of—letter or number grades:

1. Grades tend to reduce students' interest in the learning itself. One of the best-researched findings in the field of motivational psychology is that the more people are rewarded for doing something, the more they tend to lose interest in whatever they had to do to get the reward (Kohn 1993). Thus, it shouldn't be surprising that when students are told they'll need to know something for a test—or, more generally, that something they're about to do will count for a grade—they are likely to come to view that task (or book or idea) as a chore.

While it's not impossible for a student to be concerned about getting high marks and also to like what he or she is doing, the

Originally published in *High School Magazine* in 1999.

practical reality is that these two ways of thinking generally pull in opposite directions. Some research has explicitly demonstrated that a "grade orientation" and a "learning orientation" are inversely related (Beck, Rorrer-Woody, and Pierce 1991; Milton, Pollio, and Eison 1986). More strikingly, study after study has found that students—from elementary school to graduate school, and across cultures—demonstrate less interest in learning as a result of being graded (Benware and Deci 1984; Butler 1987; Butler and Nisan 1986; Grolnick and Ryan 1987; Harter and Guzman 1986; Hughes, Sullivan, and Mosley 1985; Kage 1991; Salili et al. 1976). Thus, anyone who wants to see students get hooked on words and numbers and ideas already has reason to look for other ways of assessing and describing their achievement.

2. Grades tend to reduce students' preference for challenging tasks. Students of all ages who have been led to concentrate on getting a good grade are likely to pick the easiest possible assignment if given a choice (Harter 1978; Harter and Guzman 1986; Kage 1991; Milton, Pollio, and Eison 1986). The more pressure to get an A, the less inclination to truly challenge oneself. Thus, students who cut corners may not be lazy so much as rational; they are adapting to an environment where good grades, not intellectual exploration, are what count. They might well say to us, "Hey, you told me the point here is to bring up my GPA, to get on the honor roll. Well, I'm not stupid: The easier the assignment, the more likely that I can give you what you want. So don't blame me when I try to find the easiest thing to do and end up not learning anything."

3. Grades tend to reduce the quality of students' thinking. Given that students may lose interest in what they're learning as a result of grades, it makes sense that they're also apt to think less deeply. One series of studies, for example, found that students given numerical grades were significantly less creative than those who received qualitative feedback but no grades. The more the task required creative thinking, in fact, the worse the performance of students who knew they were going to be graded. Providing students with comments in addition to a grade didn't help: The highest achievement occurred only when comments were given *instead of* numerical scores (Butler 1987; Butler 1988; Butler and Nisan 1986).

In another experiment, students told they would be graded on how well they learned a social studies lesson had more trouble understanding the main point of the text than did students who were told that no grades would be involved. Even on a measure of rote recall, the graded group remembered fewer facts a week later (Grolnick and Ryan 1987). And students who tended to think about current events in terms of what they'd need to know for a grade were less knowledgeable than their peers, even after taking other variables into account (Anderman and Johnston 1998).

More Reasons to Just Say No to Grades

The preceding three results should be enough to cause any conscientious educator to rethink the practice of giving students grades. But there's more.

Grades aren't valid, reliable, or objective. A B in English says nothing about what a student can do, what she understands, where she needs help. Moreover, the basis for that grade is as subjective as the result is uninformative. A teacher can meticulously record scores for one test or assignment after another, eventually calculating averages down to a hundredth of a percentage point, but that doesn't change the arbitrariness of each of these individual marks. Even the score on a math test is largely a reflection of how the test was written: what skills the teacher decided to assess, what kinds of questions happened to be left out, and how many points each section was "worth."

Moreover, research has long been available to confirm what all of us know: Any given assignment may well be given two different grades by two equally qualified teachers. It may even be given two different grades by a single teacher who reads it at two different times (for example, see some of the early research reviewed in Kirschenbaum, Simon, and Napier 1971). In short, what grades offer is spurious precision—a subjective rating masquerading as an objective evaluation.

Grades distort the curriculum. A school's use of letter or number grades may encourage a fact- and skill-based approach to instruction because that sort of learning is easier to score. The tail of assessment thus comes to wag the educational dog.

Grades waste a lot of time that could be spent on learning, Add up all the hours that teachers spend fussing with their grade books. Then factor in the (mostly unpleasant) conversations they have with students and their parents about grades. It's tempting to just roll our eyes when confronted with whining or wheedling, but the real problem rests with the practice of grading itself.

Grades encourage cheating. Again, we can either continue to blame and punish all the students who cheat—or we can look for the structural reasons this keeps happening. Researchers have found that the more students are led to focus on getting good grades, the more likely they are to cheat, even if they themselves regard cheating as wrong (Anderman, Griesinger, and Westerfield 1998; Milton, Pollio, and Eison 1986).

Grades spoil teachers' relationships with students. Consider this lament, which could have been offered by a teacher in your district: "I'm getting tired of running a classroom in which everything we do revolves around grades. I'm tired of being suspicious when students give me compliments, wondering whether or not they are just trying to raise their grade. I'm tired of spending so much time and energy grading your papers, when there are probably a dozen more productive and enjoyable ways for all of us to handle the evaluation of papers. I'm tired of hearing you ask me, 'Does this count?' And, heaven knows, I'm certainly tired of all those little arguments and disagreements we get into concerning marks which take so much fun out of the teaching and the learning . . ." (Kirschenbaum, Simon, and Napier 1971, p. 115).

Grades spoil students' relationships with one another. The quality of students' thinking has been shown to depend partly on the extent to which they are permitted to learn cooperatively (Johnson and Johnson 1989; Kohn 1992). Thus, the ill feelings, suspicion, and resentment generated by grades aren't just disagreeable in their own right; they interfere with learning.

The most destructive form of grading by far is that which is done "on a curve," such that the number of top grades is artificially limited: No matter how well all the students do, not all of them can get an A. Apart from the intrinsic unfairness of this arrangement, its practical effect is to teach students that others are potential obstacles to their own success. The kind of collaboration that can help all students to learn more effectively doesn't stand a chance in such an environment. Sadly, even teachers who don't explicitly grade on a curve may assume, perhaps unconsciously, that the final grades "ought to" come out looking more or less this way: a few very good grades, a few very bad grades, and the majority somewhere in the middle.

The competition that turns schooling into a quest for triumph and ruptures relationships among students doesn't only happen within classrooms, of course. The same effect is witnessed schoolwide when kids are not just rated but ranked, sending the message that the point isn't to learn, or even to perform well, but to defeat others. Some students might be motivated to improve their class rank, but that is completely different from being motivated to understand ideas. (Wise educators realize that it doesn't matter how motivated students are; what matters is *how* students are motivated. It is the type of motivation that counts, not the amount.)

Excuses and Distractions

Most of us are directly acquainted with at least some of these disturbing consequences of grades, yet we continue to reduce students to letters or numbers on a regular basis. Perhaps we've become inured to these effects and take them for granted. This is the way it's always been, we assume, and the way it has to be. It's rather like people who have spent all their lives in a terribly polluted city and have come to assume that this is just the way air looks—and that it's natural to be coughing all the time.

Oddly, when educators are shown that it doesn't have to be this way, some react with suspicion instead of relief. They want to know why you're making trouble, or they assert that you're exaggerating the negative effects of grades (it's really not so bad— cough, cough), or they dismiss proven alternatives to grading on the grounds that our school could never do what other schools have done.

The practical difficulties of abolishing letter grades are real. But the key question is whether those difficulties are seen as problems to be solved or as excuses for perpetuating the status quo. The logical response to the arguments and data summarized here is to say: "Good heavens! If even half of this is true, then it's imperative we do whatever we can, as soon as we can, to phase out traditional grading." Yet, many people begin and end with the problems of implementation, responding to all this evidence by saying, in effect, "Yeah, yeah, yeah, but we'll never get rid of grades because . . ."

It is also striking how many educators never get beyond relatively insignificant questions, such as how many tests to give, or how often to send home grade reports, or what number corresponds to what letter. Some even reserve their outrage for the possibility that too many students are ending up with good grades, a reaction that suggests stinginess with A's is being confused with intellectual rigor.

Common Objections

Let's consider the most frequently heard responses to the above arguments—which is to say, the most common objections to getting rid of grades.

First, it is said that students expect to receive grades and even seem addicted to them. This is often true; I've taught high school students who reacted to the absence of grades with what I can only describe as existential vertigo. *(Who am I if not a B+?)* But as more elementary and even some middle schools move to replace grades with more informative (and less destructive) systems of assessment, the damage doesn't begin until students get to high school. Moreover, elementary and middle schools that *haven't* changed their practices often cite the local high school as the reason they must get students used to getting grades regardless of their damaging effects—just as high schools point the finger at colleges.

Even when students arrive in high school already accustomed to grades, already primed to ask teachers, "Do we have to know this?" or "What do I have to do to get an A?", this is a sign that something is very wrong. It's more an indictment of what has happened to them in the past than an argument to keep doing it in the future.

Perhaps because of this training, grades can succeed in getting students to show up on time, hand in their work, and otherwise do what they're told. Many teachers are loath to give up what is essentially an instrument of control. But even to the extent this instrument works (which is not always), we are obliged to reflect on whether mindless compliance is really our goal. The teacher who exclaims, "These kids would blow off my course in a minute if they weren't getting a grade for it!" may be issuing a powerful indictment of his or her course. Who would be more reluctant to give up grades than a teacher who spends the period slapping transparencies on the overhead projector and lecturing endlessly at students about Romantic poets or genetic codes? Without bribes (A's) and threats (F's), students would have no reason to do such assignments. To maintain that this proves something is wrong with the kids—or that grades are simply "necessary"— suggests a willful refusal to examine one's classroom practices and assumptions about teaching and learning.

"If I can't give a child a better reason for studying than a grade on a report card, I ought to lock my desk and go home and stay there." So wrote Dorothy De Zouche, a Missouri teacher, in an article published in February . . . of 1945. But teachers who *can* give a child a better reason for studying don't need grades. Research substantiates this: When the curriculum is engaging— for example, when it involves hands-on, interactive learning activities—students who aren't graded at all perform just as well as those who are graded (Moeller and Reschke 1993).

Another objection: It is sometimes argued that students must be given grades because colleges demand them. One might reply that "high schools have no responsibility to serve colleges by performing the sorting function for them"—particularly if that process undermines learning (Krumboltz and Yeh 1996, p. 325). But in any case the premise of this argument is erroneous: Traditional grades are not mandatory for admission to colleges and universities. (See Addendum.)

Making Change

A friend of mine likes to say that people don't resist change —they resist being changed. Even terrific ideas (like moving a school from a grade orientation to a learning orientation) are guaranteed to self-destruct if they are simply forced down people's throats. The first step for an administrator, therefore, is to open up a conversation—to spend perhaps a full year just encouraging people to think and talk about the effects of (and alternatives to) traditional grades. This can happen in individual classes, as teachers facilitate discussions about how students regard grades, as well as in evening meetings with parents, or on a website—all with the help of relevant books, articles, speakers, videos, and visits to neighboring schools that are further along in this journey.

The actual process of "de-grading" can be done in stages. For example, a high school might start by freeing ninth-grade classes from grades before doing the same for upperclassmen. (Even a school that never gets beyond the first stage will have done a considerable service, giving students one full year when they can think about what they're learning instead of their GPAs.)

Another route to gradual change is to begin by eliminating only the most pernicious practices, such as grading on a curve or ranking students. Although grades, per se, may continue for a while, at least the message will be sent from the beginning that all students can do well, and that the point is to succeed rather than to beat others.

Anyone who has heard the term *authentic assessment* knows that abolishing grades doesn't mean eliminating the process of gathering information about student performance—and communicating that information to students and parents. Rather, abolishing grades opens up possibilities that are far more meaningful and constructive. These include narratives (written comments), portfolios (carefully chosen collections of students' writings and projects that demonstrate their interests, achievements, and improvement over time), student-led parent-teacher conferences, exhibitions, and other opportunities for students to show what they can do.

Of course, it's harder for a teacher to do these kinds of assessments if he or she has 150 or more students and sees each of them for forty-five to fifty-five minutes a day. But that's not an argument for continuing to use traditional grades; it's an argument for challenging these archaic remnants of a factory-oriented approach to instruction, structural aspects of high schools that are bad news for reasons that go well beyond the issue of assessment. It's an argument for looking into block scheduling, team teaching, interdisciplinary courses—and learning more about schools that have arranged things so each teacher can spend more time with fewer students (e.g., Meier 1995).

Administrators should be prepared to respond to parental concerns, some of them completely reasonable, about the prospect of edging away from grades. "Don't you value excellence?" You bet—and here's the evidence that traditional grading *undermines* excellence. "Are you just trying to spare the self-esteem of students who do poorly?" We are concerned that grades may be making things worse for such students, yes, but the problem isn't just that some kids won't get A's and will have their feelings hurt. The real problem is that almost all kids (including yours) will come to focus on grades and, as a result, their learning will be hurt.

If parents worry that grades are the only window they have into the school, we need to assure them that alternative assessments provide a far better view. But if parents don't seem to care about getting the most useful information or helping their children become more excited learners—if they demand grades for the purpose of documenting how much better their kids are than everyone else's—then we need to engage them in a discussion about whether this is a legitimate goal, and whether schools exist for the purpose of competitive credentialing or for the purpose of helping everyone to learn (Kohn 1998; Labaree 1997). Above all, we need to make sure that objections and concerns about the details don't obscure the main message, which is the demonstrated harm of traditional grading on the quality of students' learning and their interest in exploring ideas.

High school administrators can do a world of good in their districts by actively supporting efforts to eliminate conventional grading in elementary and middle schools. Working with their colleagues in these schools can help pave the way for making such changes at the secondary school level.

In the Meantime

Finally, there is the question of what classroom teachers can do while grades continue to be required. The short answer is that they should do everything within their power to make grades as invisible as possible for as long as possible. Helping students forget about grades is the single best piece of advice for those who want to create a learning-oriented classroom.

When I was teaching high school, I did a lot of things I now regret. But one policy that still seems sensible to me was saying to students on the first day of class that, while I was compelled to give them a grade at the end of the term, I could not in good conscience ever put a letter or number on anything they did during the term—and I would not do so. I would, however, write a comment—or, better, sit down and talk with them—as often as possible to give them feedback.

At this particular school I frequently faced students who had been prepared for admission to Harvard since their early childhood—a process I have come to call "Preparation H." I knew that my refusal to rate their learning might cause some students to worry about their marks all the more, or to create suspense about what would appear on their final grade reports, which of course would defeat the whole purpose. So I said that anyone who absolutely had to know what grade a given paper would get could come see me and we would figure it out together. An amazing thing happened: As the days went by, fewer and fewer students felt the need to ask me about grades. They began to be more involved with what we were learning, because I had taken responsibility as a teacher to stop pushing grades into their faces, so to speak, whenever they completed an assignment.

What I didn't do very well, however, was to get students involved in devising the criteria for excellence (what makes a math solution elegant, an experiment well designed, an essay persuasive, a story compelling) or in deciding how well their projects met those criteria. I'm afraid I unilaterally set the criteria and evaluated the students' efforts. But I have seen teachers who were more willing to give up control, more committed to helping students participate in assessment and turn that into part of the learning. Teachers who work with their students to design powerful alternatives to letter grades have a replacement ready to go when the school finally abandons traditional grading—and are able to minimize the harm of such grading in the meantime.

Addendum: Must Concerns About College Derail High School Learning?

Here is the good news: College admissions practices are not as rigid and reactionary as many people think. Here is the better news: Even when that process doesn't seem to have its priorities straight, high schools don't have to be dragged down to that level.

Sometimes it is assumed that admissions officers at the best universities are eighty-year-old fuddy-duddies peering over their spectacles and muttering about "highly irregular" applications. In truth, the people charged with making these decisions are often just a few years out of college themselves, and after making their way through a pile of interchangeable applications from 3.8-GPA, student-council-vice-president, musically accomplished hopefuls from high-powered traditional suburban high schools, they are desperate for something unconventional. Given that the most selective colleges have been known to accept home-schooled children who have never set foot in a classroom, secondary schools have more latitude than they sometimes assume. It is not widely known, for example, that hundreds of colleges and universities don't require applicants to take either the SAT or the ACT.

Admittedly, large state universities are more resistant to unconventional applications than are small private colleges simply because of economics: It takes more time, and therefore more money, for admissions officers to read meaningful application materials than it does for them to glance at a GPA or an SAT score and plug it into a formula. But I have heard of high schools approaching the admissions directors of nearby universities and saying, in effect, "We'd like to improve our school by getting rid of grades. Here's why. Will you work with us to make sure our seniors aren't penalized?" This strategy may well be successful for the simple reason that not many high schools are requesting this at present and the added inconvenience for admissions offices is likely to be negligible. Of course, if more and more high schools abandon traditional grades, then the universities will have no choice but to adapt. This is a change that high schools will have to initiate rather than waiting for colleges to signal their readiness.

At the moment, plenty of admissions officers enjoy the convenience of class ranking, apparently because they have confused being better than one's peers with being good at something; they're looking for winners rather than learners. But relatively few colleges actually insist on this practice. When a 1993 survey by the National Association of Secondary School Principals asked eleven hundred admissions officers what would happen if a high school stopped computing class rank, only 0.5 percent said the school's applicants would not be considered for admission, 4.5 percent said it would be a "great handicap," and 14.4 percent said it would be a "handicap" (Levy and Riordan 1994). In other words, it appears that the absence of class ranks would not interfere at all with students' prospects for admission to four out of five colleges.

Even more impressive, some high schools not only refuse to rank their students but refuse to give any sort of letter or number grades. Courses are all taken pass/fail, sometimes with narrative assessments of the students' performance that become part of a college application. I have spoken to representatives of each of the schools listed below, and all assure me that, year after year, their graduates are accepted into large state universities and small, highly selective colleges. *Even the complete absence of high school grades is not a barrier to college admission,* so we don't have that excuse for continuing to subject students to the harm done by traditional grading.

Any school considering the abolition of grades might want to submit a letter with each graduating student's transcript that explains why the school has chosen this course. In the meantime, feel free to contact any of these successful grade-free schools:

Metropolitan Learning Center
2033 NW Glisan
Portland, OR 97209
503/916-5737
www.pps.k12.or.us/schools/profiles/?location_id=154

Poughkeepsie Day School
39 New Hackensack Rd.
Poughkeepsie, NY 12603
914/462-7600
www.poughkeepsieday.org

School Without Walls
480 Broadway
Rochester, NY 14607
585/546-6732
www.schoolwithoutwalls.org

Alternative Community School
111 Chestnut St.
Ithaca, NY 14850
607/274-2183
www.icsd.k12.ny.us/acs/info.html

Hawthorne Valley School
330 Route 21C
Ghent, NY 12075
518/672-7092
www.hawthornevalleyschool.org

Malcolm Shabazz City High School
1601 N. Sherman Ave.
Madison, WI 53704
608/284-2440
www.madison.k12.wi.us/shabazz

Waring School
35 Standley St.
Beverly, MA 01915
978/927-8793
www.waringschool.org

Carolina Friends School
4809 Friends School Rd.
Durham, NC 27705
919/383-6602
www.cfsnc.org

Saint Ann's School
129 Pierrepont St.
Brooklyn Heights, NY 11201
718/522-1660
www.saintanns.k12.ny.us

References

Anderman, E. M., T. Griesinger, and G. Westerfield. 1998. "Motivation and Cheating During Early Adolescence." *Journal of Educational Psychology* 90: 84–93.

Anderman, E. M., and J. Johnston. 1998. "Television News in the Classroom: What Are Adolescents Learning?" *Journal of Adolescent Research* 13: 73–100.

Beck, H. P., S. Rorrer-Woody, and L. G. Pierce. 1991. "The Relations of Learning and Grade Orientations to Academic Performance." *Teaching of Psychology* 18: 35–37.

Benware, C. A., and E. L. Deci. 1984. "Quality of Learning With an Active Versus Passive Motivational Set." *American Educational Research Journal* 21: 755–65.

Butler, R. 1987. "Task-Involving and Ego-Involving Properties of Evaluation: Effects of Different Feedback Conditions on Motivational Perceptions, Interest, and Performance." *Journal of Educational Psychology* 79: 474–82.

Butler, R. 1988. "Enhancing and Undermining Intrinsic Motivation: The Effects of Task-Involving and Ego-Involving Evaluation on Interest and Performance." *British Journal of Educational Psychology* 58: 1–14.

Butler, R., and M. Nisan. 1986. "Effects of No Feedback, Task-Related Comments, and Grades on Intrinsic Motivation and Performance." *Journal of Educational Psychology* 78: 210–16.

De Zouche, D. 1945. "'The Wound Is Mortal': Marks, Honors, Unsound Activities." *The Clearing House* 19: 339–44.

Grolnick, W. S., and R. M. Ryan. 1987. "Autonomy in Children's Learning: An Experimental and Individual Difference Investigation." *Journal of Personality and Social Psychology* 52: 890–98.

Harter, S. 1978. "Pleasure Derived from Challenge and the Effects of Receiving Grades on Children's Difficulty Level Choices." *Child Development* 49: 788–99.

Harter, S., and M. E. Guzman. 1986. "The Effect of Perceived Cognitive Competence and Anxiety on Children's Problem-Solving Performance, Difficulty Level Choices, and Preference for Challenge." Unpublished manuscript, University of Denver.

Hughes, B., H. J. Sullivan, and M. L. Mosley. 1985. "External Evaluation, Task Difficulty, and Continuing Motivation." *Journal of Educational Research* 78: 210–15.

Johnson, D. W., and R. T. Johnson. 1989. *Cooperation and Competition: Theory and Research.* Edina, Minn.: Interaction Book Co.

Kage, M. 1991. "The Effects of Evaluation on Intrinsic Motivation." Paper presented at the meeting of the Japan Association of Educational Psychology, Joetsu, Japan.

Kirschenbaum, H., S. B. Simon, and R. W. Napier. 1971. *Wad-Ja-Get?: The Grading Game in American Education.* New York: Hart.

Kohn, A. 1992. *No Contest: The Case Against Competition.* Rev. ed. Boston: Houghton Mifflin.

Kohn, A. 1993. *Punished by Rewards: The Trouble with Gold Stars, Incentive Plans, A's, Praise, and Other Bribes.* Boston: Houghton Mifflin.

Kohn, A. 1998. "Only for *My* Kid: How Privileged Parents Undermine School Reform." *Phi Delta Kappan,* April: 569–77.

Krumboltz, J. D., and C. J. Yeh. 1996. "Competitive Grading Sabotages Good Teaching." *Phi Delta Kappan,* December: 324–26.

Labaree, D. F. 1997. *How to Succeed in School Without Really Learning: The Credentials Race in American Education.* New Haven, Conn.: Yale University Press.

Levy, J., and P. Riordan. 1994. *Rank-in-Class, Grade Point Average, and College Admission.* Reston, Va.: NASSP. (Available as ERIC Document 370988.)

Meier, D. 1995. *The Power of Their Ideas: Lessons for America from a Small School in Harlem.* Boston: Beacon.

Milton, O., H. R. Pollio, and J. A. Eison. 1986. *Making Sense of College Grades.* San Francisco: Jossey-Bass.

Moeller, A. J., and C. Reschke. 1993. "A Second Look at Grading and Classroom Performance: Report of a Research Study." *Modern Language Journal* 77: 163–69.

Salili, F., M. L. Maehr, R. L. Sorensen, and L. J. Fyans Jr. 1976. "A Further Consideration of the Effects of Evaluation on Motivation." *American Educational Research Journal* 13: 85–102.

10. The Dangerous Myth
of Grade Inflation

Grade inflation got started . . . in the late '60s and early '70s . . . The grades that faculty members now give . . . deserve to be a scandal.
— PROFESSOR HARVEY MANSFIELD,
HARVARD UNIVERSITY, 2001

Grades A and B are sometimes given too readily—Grade A for work of no very high merit, and Grade B for work not far above mediocrity . . . One of the chief obstacles to raising the standards of the degree is the readiness with which insincere students gain passable grades by sham work.
— REPORT OF THE COMMITTEE ON RAISING THE
STANDARD, HARVARD UNIVERSITY, 1894

Complaints about grade inflation have been around for a very long time. Every so often a fresh flurry of publicity pushes the issue to the foreground again, one example being a series of articles in the *Boston Globe* in 2001 that disclosed—in a tone normally reserved for the discovery of entrenched corruption in state government—that a lot of students at Harvard were receiving A's and being graduated with honors.

The fact that people were offering the same complaints more than a century ago puts the latest bout of harrumphing in perspective, not unlike those quotations about the disgraceful values of the younger generation that turn out to be hundreds of years old. The long history of indignation also pretty well derails any attempts to place the blame for higher grades on a residue of bleeding-heart liberal professors hired in the '60s. (Unless, of

Originally published in the *Chronicle of Higher Education* in 2002.

course, there was a similar countercultural phenomenon in the 1860s.)

Yet on campuses across America today, academe's usual requirements for supporting data and reasoned analysis have been suspended for some reason where this issue is concerned. It is largely accepted on faith that grade inflation—an upward shift in students' grade-point averages without a similar rise in achievement—exists, and that it is a bad thing. Meanwhile, the truly substantive issues surrounding grades and motivation have been obscured or ignored.

The fact is that it is hard to substantiate even the simple claim that grades have been rising. Depending on the time period we're talking about, that claim may well be false. In their book *When Hope and Fear Collide* (Jossey-Bass, 1998), Arthur Levine and Jeanette Cureton tell us that more undergraduates in 1993 reported receiving A's (and fewer reported receiving grades of C or below) compared with their counterparts in 1969 and 1976 surveys. Unfortunately, self-reports are notoriously unreliable, and the numbers become even more dubious when only a self-selected, and possibly unrepresentative, segment bothers to return the questionnaires. (One out of three failed to do so in 1993; no information is offered about the return rates in the earlier surveys.)

To get a more accurate picture of whether grades have changed over the years, one needs to look at official student transcripts. Clifford Adelman, a senior research analyst with the U.S. Department of Education, did just that, reviewing transcripts from more than three thousand institutions and reporting his results in 1995. His finding: "Contrary to the widespread lamentations, grades actually declined slightly in the last two decades." Moreover, a report released in 2002 by the National

Center for Education Statistics revealed that fully 33.5 percent of American undergraduates had a grade-point average of C or below in 1999–2000, a number that ought to quiet "all the furor over grade inflation," according to a spokesperson for the Association of American Colleges and Universities. (A review of other research suggests a comparable lack of support for claims of grade inflation at the high school level.)

However, even where grades *are* higher now as compared with then—which may well be true in the most selective institutions—that does not constitute proof that they are inflated. The burden rests with critics to demonstrate that those higher grades are undeserved, and one can cite any number of alternative explanations. Maybe students are turning in better assignments. Maybe instructors used to be too stingy with their marks and have become more reasonable. Maybe the concept of assessment itself has evolved, so that today it is more a means for allowing students to demonstrate what they know rather than for sorting them or "catching them out." (The real question, then, is why we spent so many years trying to make good students look bad.) Maybe students aren't forced to take as many courses outside their primary areas of interest in which they didn't fare as well. Maybe struggling students are now able to withdraw from a course before a poor grade appears on their transcripts. (Say what you will about that practice, it challenges the hypothesis that the grades students receive in the courses they complete are inflated.)

The bottom line: No one has ever demonstrated that students today get A's for the same work that used to receive B's or C's. We simply do not have the data to support such a claim.

Consider the most recent, determined effort by a serious source to prove that grades are inflated: "Evaluation and the Academy: Are We Doing the Right Thing?" a report released in

2002 by the American Academy of Arts and Sciences, whose senior author was Henry Rosovsky, formerly Harvard's dean of the faculty. The first argument offered in support of the proposition that students couldn't possibly deserve higher grades is that SAT scores have dropped during the same period that grades are supposed to have risen. But this is a patently inapt comparison, if only because the SAT is deeply flawed. It has never been much good even at predicting grades during the freshman year in college, to say nothing of more important academic outcomes. A four-year analysis of almost seventy-eight thousand University of California students, published in 2001 by the UC president's office, found that the test predicted only 13.3 percent of variation in freshman grades, a figure roughly consistent with hundreds of previous studies. (I outline numerous other problems with the test in chapter 8 of this volume.)

Even if one believes that the SAT is a valid and valuable exam, however, the claim that scores are dropping is a poor basis for the assertion that grades are too high. First, it is difficult to argue that a standardized test taken in high school and grades for college course work are measuring the same thing. Second, changes in aggregate SAT scores mostly reflect the proportion of the eligible population that has chosen to take the test. The American Academy's report states that average SAT scores dropped slightly from 1969 to 1993. But over that period, the pool of test-takers grew from about one-third to more than two-fifths of high school graduates—an addition of more than two hundred thousand students.

Third, a decline in overall SAT scores is hardly the right benchmark against which to measure the grades earned at Harvard or other elite institutions. Every bit of evidence I could find—including a review of the SAT scores of entering students at Harvard over the past two decades, at the nation's most selective colleges over three and even four decades, and at all private colleges since 1985—uniformly confirms a virtually linear rise in both verbal and math scores, even after correcting for the renorming of the test in the mid-1990s. To cite just one example, the latest edition of "Trends in College Admissions" reports that the average verbal SAT score of students enrolled in all private colleges rose from 543 in 1985 to 558 in 1999. Thus, those who regard SAT results as a basis for comparison should *expect* to see higher grades now rather than assume that they are inflated.

The other two arguments made by the authors of the American Academy's report rely on a similar sleight of hand. They note that more college students are now forced to take remedial courses, but they offer no reason to think that this is especially true of the relevant student population—namely, those at the most selective colleges who are now receiving A's instead of B's.

Finally, they report that more states are adding high school graduation tests and even standardized exams for admission to public universities. Yet that trend can be explained by political factors and offers no evidence of an objective decline in students' proficiency. For instance, scores on the National Assessment of Educational Progress, known as "the nation's report card" on elementary and secondary schooling, have shown very little change over the past couple of decades, and most of the change that has occurred has been for the better. As David Berliner and Bruce Biddle put it in their tellingly titled book *The Manufactured Crisis* (Addison-Wesley, 1995), the data demonstrate that "today's students are at least as well informed as students in previous generations." The latest round of public school bashing—and concomitant reliance on high-stakes testing—began with the Reagan administration's "Nation at Risk" report, featuring claims now widely viewed by researchers as exaggerated and misleading.

* * *

Beyond the absence of good evidence, the debate over grade inflation brings up knotty epistemological problems. To say that grades are not merely rising but inflated—and that they are consequently "less accurate" now, as the American Academy's report puts it—is to postulate the existence of an objectively correct evaluation of what a student (or an essay) deserves, the true grade that ought to be uncovered and honestly reported. It would be an understatement to say that this reflects a simplistic and outdated view of knowledge and of learning.

In fact, what is most remarkable is how rarely learning even figures into the discussion. The dominant disciplinary sensibility in commentaries on this topic is not that of education—an exploration of pedagogy or assessment—but rather of economics. That is clear from the very term *grade inflation,* which is, of course, just a metaphor. Our understanding is necessarily limited if we confine ourselves to the vocabulary of inputs and outputs, incentives, resource distribution, and compensation.

Suppose, for the sake of the argument, we assumed the very worst—not only that students are getting better grades than did their counterparts of an earlier generation, but that the grades are too high. What does that mean, and why does it upset some people so?

To understand grade inflation in its proper context, we must acknowledge a truth that is rarely named: The crusade against it is led by conservative individuals and organizations who regard it as analogous—or even related—to such favorite whipping boys as multicultural education, the alleged radicalism of academe, "political correctness" (a label that permits the denigration of anything one doesn't like without having to offer a reasoned objection), and too much concern about students' self-esteem. Mainstream media outlets and college administrators have allowed themselves to be put on the defensive by accusations of grade inflation, as can be witnessed when deans at Harvard plead nolo contendere and dutifully tighten their grading policies.

What are the critics assuming about the nature of students' motivation to learn, about the purpose of evaluation and of education itself? (It is surely revealing when someone reserves time and energy to complain bitterly about how many students are getting A's—as opposed to expressing concern about, say, how many students have been trained to think that the point of going to school is to get A's.)

"In a healthy university, it would not be necessary to say what is wrong with grade inflation," Harvey Mansfield asserted in an opinion article in the *Chronicle* (April 6, 2001). That, to put it gently, is a novel view of health. It seems reasonable to expect those making an argument to be prepared to defend it, and also valuable to bring their hidden premises to light. Here are the assumptions that seem to underlie the grave warnings about grade inflation:

The professor's job is to sort students for employers or graduate schools. Some are disturbed by grade inflation—or, more accurately, grade compression—because it then becomes harder to spread out students on a continuum, ranking them against one another for the benefit of postcollege constituencies. One professor asks, by way of analogy, "Why would anyone subscribe to *Consumers Digest* if every blender were rated a 'best buy'?"

But how appropriate is such a marketplace analogy? Is the professor's job to rate students like blenders for the convenience of corporations, or to offer feedback that will help students learn more skillfully and enthusiastically? (Notice, moreover, that even consumer magazines don't grade on a curve. They report the happy news if it turns out that every blender meets a reasonable set of performance criteria.)

Furthermore, the student-as-appliance approach assumes that grades provide useful information to those postcollege constituencies. Yet growing evidence—most recently in the fields of medicine and law, as cited in publications like the *Journal of the American Medical Association* and the *American Educational Research Journal*—suggests that grades and test scores do not in fact predict career success, or much of anything beyond subsequent grades and test scores.

Students should be set against one another in a race for artificially scarce rewards. "The essence of grading is exclusiveness," Mansfield said in one interview. Students "should have to compete with each other," he said in another.

In other words, even when no graduate school admissions committee pushes for students to be sorted, they ought to be sorted anyway, with grades reflecting relative standing rather than absolute accomplishment. In effect, this means that the game should be rigged so that no matter how well students do, only a few can get A's. The question guiding evaluation in such a classroom is not "How well are they learning?" but "Who's beating whom?" The ultimate purpose of good colleges, this view holds, is not to maximize success, but to ensure that there will always be losers.

A bell curve may sometimes—but only sometimes—describe the range of knowledge in a roomful of students at the beginning of a course. When it's over, though, any responsible educator hopes that the results would skew drastically to the right, meaning that most students learned what they hadn't known before. Thus, in their important study *Making Sense of College Grades* (Jossey-Bass, 1986), Ohmer Milton, Howard Pollio, and James Eison write, "It is not a symbol of rigor to have grades fall into a 'normal' distribution; rather, it is a symbol of failure—failure to teach well, failure to test well, and failure to have any influence at all on the intellectual lives of students."

Making sure that students are continually re-sorted, with excellence turned into an artificially scarce commodity, is almost perverse.

What does relative success signal about student performance in any case? The number of peers that a student has bested tells us little about how much she knows and is able to do. Moreover, such grading policies may create a competitive climate that is counterproductive for winners and losers alike, to the extent that it discourages a free exchange of ideas and a sense of community that's conducive to exploration.

Harder is better (or higher grades mean lower standards). Compounding the tendency to confuse excellence with victory is a tendency to confuse quality with difficulty—as evidenced in the accountability fad that has elementary and secondary education in its grip just now, with relentless talk of "rigor" and "raising the bar." The same confusion shows up in higher education when professors pride themselves not on the intellectual depth and value of their classes but merely on how much reading they assign, how hard their tests are, how rarely they award good grades, and so on. "You're going to have to *work* in here!" they announce, with more than a hint of machismo and self-congratulation.

Some people might defend that posture on the grounds that students will perform better if A's are harder to come by. In fact, the evidence on this question is decidedly mixed. Stringent grading sometimes has been shown to boost short-term retention as measured by multiple-choice exams—never to improve understanding or promote interest in learning. An analysis released in 2000 by Julian R. Betts and Jeff Grogger, professors of economics at the University of California at San Diego and at Los Angeles, respectively, found that tougher grading was initially correlated with higher test scores. But the long-term effects were negligible—with the exception of minority students, for whom the effects were negative.

It appears that something more than an empirical hypothesis is behind the "harder is better" credo, particularly when it is set up as a painfully false dichotomy: Those easy-grading professors are too lazy to care, or too worried about how students will evaluate them, or overly concerned about their students' self-esteem, whereas *we* are the last defenders of what used to matter in the good old days. High standards! Intellectual honesty! No free lunch!

The American Academy's report laments an absence of "candor" about this issue. Let us be candid, then. Those who grumble about undeserved grades sometimes exude a cranky impatience with—or even contempt for—the late adolescents and young adults who sit in their classrooms. Many people teaching in higher education, after all, see themselves primarily as researchers and regard teaching as an occupational hazard, something they're not very good at, were never trained for, and would rather avoid. It would be interesting to examine the correlation between one's view of teaching (or of students) and the intensity of one's feelings about grade inflation. Someone also might want to examine the personality profiles of those who become infuriated over the possibility that someone, somewhere, got an A without having earned it.

Grades motivate. With the exception of orthodox behaviorists, psychologists have come to realize that people can exhibit qualitatively different kinds of motivation: intrinsic, in which the task itself is seen as valuable, and extrinsic, in which the task is just a means to the end of gaining a reward or escaping a punishment. The two are not only distinct but often inversely related. Scores of studies have demonstrated, for example, that the more people are rewarded, the more they come to lose interest in whatever had to be done in order to get the reward. (That conclusion is essentially reaffirmed by the latest major meta-analysis on the topic: a review of 128 studies, published in 1999 by Edward L. Deci, Richard Koestner, and Richard Ryan.)

Those unfamiliar with that basic distinction, let alone the supporting research, may be forgiven for pondering how to "motivate" students, then concluding that grades are often a good way of doing so, and consequently worrying about the impact of inflated grades. The problem is that a focus on grades creates, or at least perpetuates, an extrinsic orientation that is likely to undermine the love of learning we are presumably seeking to promote.

Three robust findings emerge from the empirical literature on the subject: Students who are given grades, or for whom grades are made particularly salient, tend to display less interest in what they are doing, fare worse on meaningful measures of learning, and avoid more challenging tasks when given the opportunity—as compared with those in a nongraded comparison group. College instructors cannot help noticing, and presumably being disturbed by, such consequences, but they may lapse into blaming students ("grade grubbers") rather than understanding the systemic sources of the problem. A focus on whether too many students are getting A's suggests a tacit endorsement of grades that predictably produces just such a mindset in students.

These fundamental questions are almost completely absent from discussions of grade inflation. The American Academy's report takes exactly one sentence—with no citations—to dismiss the argument that "lowering the anxiety over grades leads to better learning," ignoring the fact that much more is involved than anxiety. It is a matter of why a student learns, not only how much stress he feels. The meaningful contrast is not between an A and a B or C, but between an extrinsic and an intrinsic focus.

Precisely because that is true, a reconsideration of grade

inflation leads us to explore alternatives to our (often unreflective) use of grades. Narrative comments and other ways by which faculty members can communicate their evaluations can be far more informative than letter or number grades, and much less destructive. Indeed, some colleges—for example, Hampshire, Evergreen State, Alverno, and New College of Florida—have eliminated grades entirely, as a critical step toward *raising* intellectual standards. Even the American Academy's report acknowledges that "relatively undifferentiated course grading has been a traditional practice in many graduate schools for a very long time." Has that policy produced lower quality teaching and learning? Quite the contrary: Many people say they didn't begin to explore ideas deeply and passionately until graduate school began and the importance of grades diminished significantly.

If the continued use of grades rests on nothing more than tradition ("We've always done it that way"), a faulty understanding of motivation, or excessive deference to graduate-school admissions committees, then it may be time to balance those factors against the demonstrated harms of getting students to chase A's. Ohmer Milton and his colleagues discovered—and others have confirmed—that a "grade orientation" and a "learning orientation" on the part of students tend to be inversely related. That raises the disturbing possibility that some colleges are institutions of higher learning in name only, because the paramount question for students is not "What does this mean?" but "Do we have to know this?"

A grade-oriented student body is an invitation for the administration and faculty to ask hard questions: What unexamined assumptions keep traditional grading in place? What forms of assessment might be less destructive? How can professors minimize the salience of grades in their classrooms, so long as grades must still be given? And: If the artificial inducement of grades disappeared, what sort of teaching strategies might elicit authentic interest in a course?

To engage in this sort of inquiry, to observe real classrooms, and to review the relevant research is to arrive at one overriding conclusion: The real threat to excellence isn't grade inflation at all; it's grades.

NOTE: *For a discussion of the research on which this article is based, please see www.alfiekohn.org/teaching/gisources.htm.*

11. Five Reasons to Stop Saying "Good Job!"

Hang out at a playground, visit a school, or show up at a child's birthday party, and there's one phrase you can count on hearing repeatedly: "Good job!" Even tiny infants are praised for smacking their hands together ("Good clapping!"). Many of us blurt out these judgments of our children to the point that it has become almost a verbal tic.

Plenty of books and articles advise us against relying on punishment, from spanking to forcible isolation ("time out"). Occasionally someone will even ask us to rethink the practice of bribing children with stickers or food. But you'll have to look awfully hard to find a discouraging word about what is euphemistically called positive reinforcement.

Lest there be any misunderstanding, the point here is not to call into question the importance of supporting and encouraging children, the need to love them and hug them and help them feel good about themselves. Praise, however, is a different story entirely. Here's why.

1. Manipulating children. Suppose you offer a verbal reward to reinforce the behavior of a two-year-old who eats without spilling, or a five-year-old who cleans up her art supplies. Who benefits from this? Is it possible that telling kids they've done a good job may have less to do with their emotional needs than with our convenience?

Rheta DeVries, a professor of education at the University of Northern Iowa, refers to this as "sugar-coated control." Very much like tangible rewards—or, for that matter, punishments—it's a way of doing something *to* children to get them to comply with our wishes. It may be effective at producing this result (at

Originally published in *Young Children* in 2001.

least for a while), but it's very different from working *with* kids —for example, by engaging them in conversation about what makes a classroom (or family) function smoothly, or how other people are affected by what we have done—or failed to do. The latter approach is not only more respectful but more likely to help kids become thoughtful people.

The reason praise can work in the short run is that young children are hungry for our approval. But we have a responsibility not to exploit that dependence for our own convenience. A "Good job!" to reinforce something that makes our lives a little easier can be an example of taking advantage of children's dependence. Kids may also come to feel manipulated by this, even if they can't quite explain why.

2. Creating praise junkies. To be sure, not every use of praise is a calculated tactic to control children's behavior. Sometimes we compliment kids just because we're genuinely pleased by what they've done. Even then, however, it's worth looking more closely. Rather than bolstering a child's self-esteem, praise may increase kids' dependence on us. The more we say, "I like the way you . . ." or "Good _____ing," the more kids come to rely on *our* evaluations, *our* decisions about what's good and bad, rather than learning to form their own judgments. It leads them to measure their worth in terms of what will lead *us* to smile and dole out some more approval.

Mary Budd Rowe, a researcher at the University of Florida, discovered that students who were praised lavishly by their teachers were more tentative in their responses, more apt to answer in a questioning tone of voice ("Um, seven?"). They tended to back off from an idea they had proposed as soon as an adult disagreed with them. And they were less likely to persist with difficult tasks or share their ideas with other students.

In short, "Good job!" doesn't reassure children; ultimately, it makes them feel less secure. It may even create a vicious circle such that the more we slather on the praise, the more kids seem to need it, so we praise them some more. Sadly, some of these kids will grow into adults who continue to need someone else to pat them on the head and tell them whether what they did was OK. Surely this is not what we want for our daughters and sons.

3. Stealing a child's pleasure. Apart from the issue of dependence, a child deserves to take delight in her accomplishments, to feel pride in what she's learned how to do. She also deserves to decide when to feel that way. Every time we say, "Good job!", though, we're telling a child how to feel.

To be sure, there are times when our evaluations are appropriate and our guidance is necessary—especially with toddlers and preschoolers. But a constant stream of value judgments is neither necessary nor useful for children's development. Unfortunately, we may not have realized that "Good job!" is just as much an evaluation as "Bad job!" The most notable feature of a positive judgment isn't that it's positive, but that it's a judgment. And people, including kids, don't like being judged.

I cherish the occasions when my daughter manages to do something for the first time, or does something better than she's ever done it before. But I try to resist the knee-jerk tendency to say, "Good job!" because I don't want to dilute her joy. I want her to share her pleasure with me, not look to me for a verdict. I want her to exclaim, "I did it!" (which she often does) instead of asking me uncertainly, "Was that good?"

4. Losing interest. "Good painting!" may get children to keep painting for as long as we keep watching and praising. But, warns Lilian Katz, one of the country's leading authorities on early childhood education, "once attention is withdrawn, many kids won't touch the activity again." Indeed, an impressive body of scientific research has shown that the more we reward people for doing something, the more they tend to lose interest in whatever they had to do to get the reward. Now the point isn't to draw, to read, to think, to create—the point is to get the goody, whether it's an ice cream, a sticker, or a "Good job!"

In a troubling study conducted by Joan Grusec at the University of Toronto, young children who were frequently praised for displays of generosity tended to be slightly *less* generous on an everyday basis than other children were. Every time they had heard "Good sharing!" or "I'm so proud of you for helping," they became a little less interested in sharing or helping. Those actions came to be seen not as something valuable in their own right but as something they had to do to get that reaction again from an adult. Generosity became a means to an end.

Does praise motivate kids? Sure. It motivates kids to get praise. Alas, that's often at the expense of commitment to whatever they were doing that prompted the praise.

5. Reducing achievement. As if it weren't bad enough that "Good job!" can undermine independence, pleasure, and interest, it can also interfere with how good a job children actually do. Researchers keep finding that kids who are praised for doing well at a creative task tend to stumble at the next task—and they don't do as well as children who weren't praised to begin with.

Why does this happen? Partly because the praise creates *pressure* to "keep up the good work" that gets in the way of doing so. Partly because their *interest* in what they're doing may have declined. Partly because they become less likely to take *risks*—a prerequisite for creativity—once they start thinking about how to keep those positive comments coming.

More generally, "Good job!" is a remnant of an approach to psychology that reduces all of human life to behaviors that can be seen and measured. Unfortunately, this ignores the thoughts, feelings, and values that lie behind behaviors. For example, a child may share a snack with a friend as a way of attracting praise, or as a way of making sure the other child has enough to eat. Praise for sharing ignores these different motives. Worse, it actually promotes the less desirable motive by making children more likely to fish for praise in the future.

Once you start to see praise for what it is—and what it does—these constant little evaluative eruptions from adults start to produce the same effect as fingernails being dragged down a blackboard. You begin to root for a child to give his teachers or parents a taste of their own treacle by turning around to them and saying (in the same saccharine tone of voice), "Good praising!"

Still, it's not an easy habit to break. It can seem strange, at least at first, to stop praising; it can feel as though you're being chilly or withholding something. But that, it soon becomes clear, suggests that *we praise more because we need to say it than because children need to hear it.* Whenever that's true, it's time to rethink what we're doing.

What kids do need is unconditional support, love with no strings attached. That's not just different from praise—it's the *opposite* of praise. "Good job!" is conditional. It means we're offering attention and acknowledgment and approval for jumping through our hoops, for doing things that please us.

This point, you'll notice, is very different from a criticism that some people offer to the effect that we give kids too much approval, or give it too easily. They recommend that we become more miserly with our praise and demand that kids "earn" it. But the real problem isn't that children expect to be praised for everything they do these days. It's that *we're* tempted to take shortcuts,

to manipulate kids with rewards instead of explaining and helping them to develop needed skills and good values.

So what's the alternative? That depends on the situation,
but whatever we decide to say instead has to be offered in the
context of genuine affection and love for who kids are rather
than for what they've done. When unconditional support is present, "Good job!" isn't necessary; when it's absent, "Good job!"
won't help.

If we're praising positive actions as a way of discouraging misbehavior, this is unlikely to be effective for long. Even when it
works, we can't really say the child is now "behaving himself";
it would be more accurate to say the praise is behaving him.
The alternative is to work *with* the child, to figure out the reasons
he's acting that way. We may have to reconsider our own requests
rather than just looking for a way to get kids to obey. (Instead of
using "Good job!" to get a four-year-old to sit quietly through
a long class meeting or family dinner, perhaps we should ask
whether it's reasonable to expect a child to do so.)

We also need to bring kids in on the process of making decisions. If a child is doing something that disturbs others, then sitting down with her later and asking, "What do you think we can
do to solve this problem?" will likely be more effective than bribes
or threats. It also helps a child learn how to solve problems and
teaches that her ideas and feelings are important. Of course, this
process takes time and talent, care and courage. Tossing off a
"Good job!" when the child acts in the way we deem appropriate
takes none of those things, which helps to explain why "doing to"
strategies are a lot more popular than "working with" strategies.

And what can we say when kids just do something impressive? Consider three possible responses:

Say nothing. Some people insist a helpful act must be "reinforced" because, secretly or unconsciously, they believe it was a fluke. If children are basically evil, then they have to be given an artificial reason for being nice (namely, to get a verbal reward). But if that cynicism is unfounded—and a lot of research suggests that it is—then praise may not be necessary.

Say what you saw. A simple, evaluation-free statement ("You put your shoes on by yourself" or even just "You did it") tells your child that you noticed. It also lets her take pride in what she did. In other cases, a more elaborate description may make sense. If your child draws a picture, you might provide feedback—not judgment—about what you noticed: "This mountain is huge!" "Boy, you sure used a lot of purple today!"

If a child does something caring or generous, you might gently draw his attention to the effect of his action *on the other person:* "Look at Abigail's face! She seems pretty happy now that you gave her some of your snack." This is completely different from praise, where the emphasis is on how *you* feel about her sharing.

Talk less, ask more. Even better than descriptions are questions. Why tell him what part of his drawing impressed *you* when you can ask him what *he* likes best about it? Asking "What was the hardest part to draw?" or "How did you figure out how to make the feet the right size?" is likely to nourish his interest in drawing. Saying "Good job!", as we've seen, may have exactly the opposite effect.

This doesn't mean that all compliments, all thank-you's, all expressions of delight are harmful. We need to consider our *motives* for what we say (a genuine expression of enthusiasm is better than a desire to manipulate the child's future behavior) as well as the actual *effects* of doing so. Are our reactions helping the child to feel a sense of control over her life—or to constantly look to us for approval? Are they helping her to become more excited about what she's doing in its own right—or turning it into something she just wants to get through in order to receive a pat on the head?

It's not a matter of memorizing a new script, but of keeping in mind our long-term goals for our children and watching for the effects of what we say. The bad news is that the use of positive reinforcement really isn't so positive. The good news is that you don't have to evaluate in order to encourage.

Four: Moral, Social, and Psychological Questions

12. Constant Frustration and Occasional Violence: The Legacy of American High Schools

In the wake of the recent string of high school shootings, many people are desperate to find a silver lining, a way to wring hope from tragedy. At least now things will have to change, some observers might declare grimly. At least now there is no escaping the need to take a good hard look at American secondary education. Unfortunately, though, if history is any guide, that hard look will likely turn out to be short-sighted or misdirected: The point will be missed, and the responses that follow might even make things worse.

If that sounds overly pessimistic, consider the American penchant for ignoring the structural causes of problems. We prefer the simplicity and satisfaction of holding individuals responsible for whatever happens: crime, poverty, school failure, what have you. Thus, even when one high school crisis is followed by another, we concentrate on the particular people involved—their values, their character, their personal failings—rather than asking whether something about the system in which these students find themselves might also need to be addressed.

To raise this criticism is not to deny that people bear some responsibility for their actions. Nor is it to ignore the fact that there was something wrong with the kids at Columbine High School (and elsewhere) who murdered their classmates. Nevertheless, it is as naive as it is convenient to assume that the trouble resides exclusively within the heads of the killers.

Even when we do try to consider other causes, we tend to concentrate on factors that have nothing to do with our education

Originally published in *American School Board Journal* in 1999.

system—as though we weren't faced with high school shootings so much as shootings that just happened to take place in high schools. On one level, this is understandable. Ready access to guns, combined with a culture steeped in violence,[1] might be the only ingredients necessary to get from Point A (individual psychopathology) to Point B (a bloodbath). But again we must ask: Is it possible that something about our schools might also play a role? We need to steer between too narrow an analysis, in which we focus only on the individuals involved, and too broad an analysis, in which we focus only on "American culture."

As citizens, you and I might believe the most urgent task is to make it harder for young people to get hold of guns. But as people who are professionally involved with the schools, we might also want to cast a critical eye on how students are being educated. A decade ago, Deborah Meier remarked that American high schools are "peculiar institutions designed as though intended to drive kids to the edge of their sanity."[2] That might have seemed an exaggeration before Littleton (and Jonesboro and Springfield and West Paducah . . .), but today her observation deserves to be taken seriously. We need to consider what it's really like, from the student's point of view, to spend three or four years in a typical high school.

In an illuminating passage, Linda Darling-Hammond, professor of education at Stanford University, argued that

> Many well-known adolescent difficulties are not intrinsic to the teenage years but are related to the mismatch between adolescents' developmental needs and the kinds of experiences most junior high and high schools provide. When students need close affiliation, they experience large depersonalized schools; when they need to develop autonomy, they experience few opportunities for choice

and punitive approaches to discipline; when they need expansive cognitive challenges and opportunities to demonstrate their competence, they experience work focused largely on the memorization of facts . . .[3]

Read that paragraph again, slowly. It is not a casual indictment, but an evaluation based on a careful summary of what psychologists have identified as key human needs.[4] All of us yearn for a sense of relatedness or belonging, a feeling of being connected to others. All of us need to experience ourselves as self-determining, to be able to make decisions about the things that affect us. And all of us seek opportunities to feel effective, to learn new things that matter to us and find (or create) answers to personally meaningful questions. If anything, these needs are most pronounced, most urgent, for adolescents. Yet Darling-Hammond is absolutely right: American high schools not only fail to meet those needs but make a mockery of them.

What could be worse, for kids who desperately desire a feeling of connection, than to plop them down in a giant factory of a school, a huge, seemingly uncaring place where they feel invisible, anonymous, lost? (Those are the exact words many students use to describe their situation to anyone who bothers to ask.) It's not that most teachers are indifferent or sadistic people; it's that something is seriously dysfunctional about the structure of high school. Too many people are thrown together, and too little time at a stretch is provided for any subset of them to come to know one another well. From early every weekday morning until well into the afternoon, it is rare for students to have much meaningful contact with adults—or even with one another. Moreover, any sense of community that does manage to develop is snuffed out by practices that set kids against one another. When students must compete—when, for example, they are not only rated but ranked—the lesson each learns is that everyone else is an obstacle to one's own success.[5]

What could be worse, for kids who need to be able to make decisions and feel some control over their lives, than to make them spend their days following other people's rules, to tell them what to read, where to go, what to do? In many ways, secondary schools are even more controlling than elementary schools, with less opportunity for student participation. How logical is it to expect that teenagers who have been coerced into following directions will develop into responsible decision-makers? The average high school is terrific preparation for adult life—as long as that life is led in a totalitarian society.

Finally, what could be worse, for kids who need to make sense of themselves and the world, than to treat them as passive receptacles into which facts are poured? They are made to sit at separate desks while a stream of details about sonnets or binomial equations washes over them. Rather than being invited to pursue projects that seem relevant and engaging, they are required to slog through tedious textbooks, memorizing what they think they will need for the next exam. Rather than coming to understand ideas in depth, they are exposed superficially to a vast amount of material during forty-five- or fifty-minute periods. When students predictably respond to all this by tuning out, or acting out, or dropping out, we promptly blame *them* for not working hard enough. (As bad as it is, this situation is now becoming even worse as high-stakes exams and misguided demands for "accountability" and "tougher standards" squeeze out whatever intellectual exploration had somehow survived.[6] The more that high schools are transformed into test-prep centers—fact factories, if you will—the more alienated we can expect students to become.)

Does it not seem plausible that these gross disparities between what students need and what they get in high school might be related to the acts of terrible violence that occur there? Foreclose the possibility of a meaningful community, and students will create something to which they can belong, even if it is the kind of group that we find disturbing. Make students feel powerless, and the need for autonomy might express itself in antisocial ways. Treat students as interchangeable and anonymous, and occasionally someone will do dreadful things to attract attention and make his mark.

This is, intentionally, a serious indictment of the American high school. How might defenders of the status quo respond?

CHALLENGE: You haven't convinced me that kids have a fundamental need to feel related, autonomous, and competent.

REPLY: Anyone is welcome to amend this particular list of basic needs or propose another list in its place. But it's not as though American high schools are trying to meet a different set of needs. The problem is that, as a rule, they are not designed to meet students' needs at all.

CHALLENGE: Even if the summary of needs is basically accurate, high schools really aren't so bad at meeting them. Your description is exaggerated.

REPLY: Anyone who thinks that most students in most high schools don't feel alienated, powerless, and unengaged need only (1) think back to his or her own years in high school, because very little has changed since then; (2) read some of the best contemporary accounts of high school life, such as Ted Sizer's *Horace's Compromise* and Linda McNeil's *Contradictions of Control;* or (3) follow a high school student around for at least one full day.

CHALLENGE: Maybe high schools are dreadful places, but it's not clear what we can do to improve them.

REPLY: The education literature is brimming with specific suggestions. For example, Darling-Hammond cites research showing that "teenagers who stay in more nurturing settings where they encounter less departmentalization, fewer teachers, and smaller groups experience higher achievement, attendance, and self-confidence than those who enter large impersonal departmentalized secondary schools."[7] High school reformers, including those affiliated with the Coalition of Essential Schools,[8] have developed (and sometimes even implemented) proposals for transforming schools into places that are both more welcoming and more intellectually engaging. These ideas range from setting up small advisory groups to replacing traditional grades and tests with "exhibitions" of meaningful learning.

CHALLENGE: It's not easy to implement these changes.

REPLY: Indeed, I often meet students, parents, teachers, and principals who are committed to educational renewal but lack the power to restructure schools, to replace existing practices with those that are more need-fulfilling. Frustrated, they urge me to "talk to the school board members and the superintendents." Hence this article.

Of course, even those who have more authority to make change do not operate in a vacuum. They may face state legislators and newspaper reporters who don't know the difference between intellectual quality and high standardized test scores, with the result that the former is sacrificed in a quest for the latter. They may face college admissions officers whose criteria are disturbingly narrow. (One wag suggests that teachers ought to just issue a formal declaration of surrender to the Educational Testing Service and be done with it.) They may face parents who reflexively oppose meaningful reform, sometimes seeming to say, "Hey, if the traditional approach was bad enough for me, it's bad enough for my kid."

Still, the constraints faced by school board members and other key players cannot become an excuse for inaction. The stakes are too high; the damage done by the present system is too great. Education policymakers must lead as well as follow, and leading entails educating members of the community. They must also recognize that the usual explanations can go only so far in rationalizing current practices. For example, no college admissions office demands huge high schools, or short class periods, or an absence of opportunities for students to make decisions. Some secondary schools have created opportunities for more thoughtful learning—and have even eliminated letter grades entirely without jeopardizing students' chances for acceptance into selective colleges and universities. (See pp. 88–90.)

Meanwhile, school leaders can invite parents to reflect on their long-term goals for their children. What do we want them to be? How do we want them to turn out? Parents can be helped to understand that the characteristics they list (responsible, caring, happy, creative, lifelong learners, and so on) are more difficult to promote in traditional schools. The knee-jerk demand for textbooks, honor rolls, and other familiar practices might even make it less likely that students will develop the features valued by their parents and others in the community.

Unhappily, many school officials fail to grapple with these key issues or commit themselves to meaningful change. In fact, some throw fuel on the fire, unwittingly making things worse by responding to signs of student distress with even harsher discipline. Consistent with the tendency to ignore the structural causes of problems, they seem to think sheer force can be employed to make the bad stuff disappear: Tell the kids what to wear, subject them to drug tests, announce a "zero-tolerance"[9] policy. Punishment is based on the premise that making people suffer for doing something wrong will lead them to see the error of their ways. If punishment proves ineffective, then it is assumed that *more* punishment—along with tighter regulations and less trust—will certainly do the trick.

The shootings at Columbine provoked a general panic in which hundreds of students across the country were arrested, according to *Education Week,* while "countless others were suspended or expelled for words or deeds perceived as menacing." The fear here is understandable: Could our district, too, be incubating killers? But there is a critical distinction that virtually no one has made: We need to understand the difference between *overreaction,* such as closing down a school to search for bombs after a student makes an off-hand joke, and *destructive reaction,* such as relying on a policy of coercion to make things safer.

Experience should tell us that cracking down on students (with more suspensions or other punitive strategies) will not only fail to solve the problem but might exacerbate it. Even in those cases where a student's actions pose a significant risk to the safety of others, the first question for every school board member and administrator should not be "Have we used sufficient force to stamp out this threat?" but "What have we done to address the underlying issues here? How can we transform our schools into places that meet students' needs so there is less chance that someone will be moved to lash out in fury?"

Although I have suggested the possibility of a link between the nature of school, on the one hand, and acts of violence that take place in school, on the other, I can't be sure that one causes the other. But perhaps we should take a step back and ask how important it is to establish such a connection. After all, the case for high school reform shouldn't have to be made on the basis of gunfire. Even if no one was ever shot on school grounds, the daily frustration and steady alienation experienced by the overwhelming majority of high school students offer reason enough to rethink what their schools are like. The desperation of the masses might be expressed more quietly, but if the environment in which they find themselves is stultifying, that is an invitation for us to take action. Or, to put it differently, a lack of violence doesn't imply that all is well, just as the students who don't make trouble for the teacher aren't necessarily the "good" kids—just the docile kids.

The undeniable fact is that we don't always respect the everyday experiences and needs of all students. Some teachers derive their professional pride from the occasional kid who goes on to become famous. (This, as Deborah Meier has observed, reflects a powerfully antidemocratic sensibility. It says education is about winnowing and selecting rather than providing something of value for everyone.) Some parents essentially mortgage their children's present to the future, sacrificing what might bring meaning or enjoyment—or even produce higher quality learning—in a ceaseless effort to prepare their children for college; they are not raising a child so much as a résumé on legs. And some policymakers see students mostly as test scores, valuing only those who get the best numbers—and therefore not really valuing any of them.

More than half a century ago, John Dewey lamented that "the conditions still too largely prevailing in the school—the size of the classes, the load of work, and so on—make it difficult to carry on the educative process in any genuinely cooperative democratic way."[10] The fact that this situation is even worse today just might be connected to the tragic events we've observed recently in some of those schools. In any case, it represents a tragedy in itself.

Notes

1. To talk honestly about a culture steeped in violence is not just to condemn violent entertainment. Movies and videogames that turn killing into sport are popular around the world, sad to say, including in countries with very low murder rates. The United States, however, is one of the few industrialized countries that still puts criminals to death. It is a nation where the use of physical violence on children is still defended as a legitimate form of discipline, even in many schools. And it is a nation that has invaded or bombed dozens of others over the decades. Any child growing up here, even one who has never seen a Schwarzenegger or Stallone film, receives a constant stream of messages to the effect that hurting and killing are socially acceptable, at least under some conditions.

Schools could, but rarely do, help students reflect on capital punishment, corporal punishment, and the militarism that lies behind the rhetoric of U.S. foreign policy. They could invite discussion about why millions of people make a fetish about the right to own devices whose only purpose is to injure or kill. More broadly, they could, but rarely do, encourage students to think critically about our society rather than leading them to accept our institutions and ideologies as "just the way life is."

2. "The Kindergarten Tradition in the High School," in *Progressive Education for the 1990s*, ed. Kathe Jervis and Carol Montag (New York: Teachers College Press, 1991), p. 138.

3. *The Right to Learn: A Blueprint for Creating Schools That Work* (San Francisco: Jossey-Bass, 1997), p. 122. She adds that when students "need to build self-confidence and a healthy identity, they experience tracking that explicitly labels many of them as academically deficient"—an equally disturbing situation that I lack the space to address here.

4. For example, see the work of Edward Deci and Richard Ryan.

5. A generally competitive culture often goes hand in hand with an ugly kind of social stratification. Columbine High School, like many others, was characterized not only by the size of its student body (nearly two thousand) but by a tendency on the part of students and staff alike to deify athletes. Some of these sports stars taunted other students mercilessly "while school authorities looked the other way." (See Lorraine Adams and Dale Russakoff, "Dissecting Columbine's Cult of the Athlete," *Washington Post*, June 12, 1999, p. A1. Also see

Bernard Lefkowitz, *Our Guys: The Glen Ridge Rape and the Secret Life of the Perfect Suburb* [Berkeley: University of California Press, 1997].)

6. For more on this topic, see Alfie Kohn, *The Schools Our Children Deserve: Moving Beyond Traditional Classrooms and "Tougher Standards"* (Boston: Houghton Mifflin, 1999).

7. Darling-Hammond, *The Right to Learn*, p. 122.

8. For more information, contact the coalition at 1814 Franklin Street, Suite 700, Oakland, CA 94612, (510) 433–1451, or at www.essentialschools.org.

9. For an excellent discussion of this topic, see Russ Skiba and Reece Peterson, "The Dark Side of Zero Tolerance: Can Punishment Lead to Safe Schools?" *Phi Delta Kappan*, January 1999, pp. 372–76, 381–82.

10. John Dewey's comment appears in *Dewey on Education*, ed. Martin S. Dworkin (New York: Teachers College Press, 1959), p. 130.

13. September 11

Some events seem momentous when they occur but gradually fade from consciousness, overtaken by fresh headlines and the distractions of daily life. Only once in a great while does something happen that will be taught by future historians. Just such an incident occurred on September 11, 2001. The deadly attacks on New York and Washington have left us groping for support, for words, for a way to make meaning and recover our balance.

Almost thirty years ago, my father suffered a serious heart attack at the age of forty-two. I remember how he smiled up at me weakly from his hospital bed and made a joke that wasn't a joke. "I guess I'm not as immortal as I thought I was," he murmured. On September 11 we all suffered an attack that stole from us, individually and collectively, our sense of invincibility. Our airplanes can be turned into missiles. Our skyline can be altered. We can't be sure that our children are safe.

It is unimaginable to me that people could patiently plan such carnage, could wake up each morning, eat breakfast, and spend the day preparing to destroy thousands of innocent lives along with their own. But while the particulars seem unfathomable, the attack itself had a context and perhaps a motive that are perfectly comprehensible—and especially important for educators to grasp.

The historical record suggests that the United States has no problem with terrorism as long as its victims don't live here or look like most of us. In the last couple of decades alone, we have bombed Libya, invaded Grenada, attacked Panama, and shelled Lebanon—killing civilians in each instance. We created and funded an army of terrorists to overthrow the elected government of Nicaragua, and when the World Court ruled that we

Originally published in *Rethinking Schools* in 2002.

must stop, we simply rejected the court's authority. We engineered coups in Iran, Zaire, Guatemala, and Chile (the last of which coincidentally also took place on September 11).

In 1991 we killed more than a hundred thousand men, women, and children in Iraq, deliberately wiping out electricity and water supplies with the result that tens of thousands of civilians died from malnutrition and disease. We continue to vigorously defend (and subsidize) Israel's brutal treatment of Palestinians, which has been condemned by human rights organizations and virtually every other nation on the planet. We have aided vile tyrants, including some who later turned against us: Manuel Noriega, Saddam Hussein, and, yes, Osama bin Laden (when his opposition to the Soviets served our purposes). We are not the only nation that has done such things, but we are the most powerful and, therefore, arguably the most dangerous.

Does any of this justify an act of terrorism against us? No. Our history may help to explain, but decidedly does not excuse, the taking of innocent lives. Nothing could. By the same token, though, the September attack does not justify a retaliatory war launched by our government that takes innocent lives abroad. Early polls showed overwhelming American support for revenge, even for killing civilians in Muslim countries. If this seems understandable given what happened, then the same must be said about the animosity of our attackers, some of whom may have suffered personally from U.S.-sponsored violence. Understandable in both cases—and excusable in neither.

And so we come to our role as educators. There are excellent resources for helping students to reflect deeply about these specific issues, such as the website www.teachingforchange.org/Sept11.htm. But our broader obligation is to address what writer Martin Amis described as Americans' chronic "deficit of empathy for the sufferings of people far away." Schools should help children locate themselves in widening circles of care that extend beyond self, beyond country, to all humanity.

Likewise, education must be about developing the skills and disposition to question the official story, to view with skepticism the stark us-against-them (or us good, them bad) portrait of the world and the accompanying dehumanization of others that helps to explain that empathy deficit. Students should also be able to recognize dark historical parallels in the president's rhetoric, and to notice what is not being said or shown on the news.

One detail of the tragedy carries a striking pedagogical relevance. Official announcements in the south tower of the World Trade Center repeatedly instructed everyone in the building to stay put, which posed an agonizing choice: Follow the official directive or disobey and evacuate. Here we find a fresh reason to ask whether we are teaching students to think for themselves or simply to do what they're told.

Ultimately, though, the standard by which to measure our schools is the extent to which the next generation comes to understand—and fully embrace—this simple truth: The life of someone who lives in Kabul or Baghdad is worth no less than the life of someone in New York or from our neighborhood.

14. A Fresh Look at Abraham Maslow

Abraham Maslow was a bundle of paradoxes. After writing a popular text on abnormal psychology, he turned to—and virtually initiated—the serious study of healthy people. He apprenticed under some of the leading behaviorists, he was psychoanalyzed for years, yet he shaped a Third Force in psychology that explicitly repudiated behaviorism and psychoanalysis. The anecdotes compiled by his biographer (Hoffman 1988) suggest a man both gentle and intolerant, timid and arrogant. He dreamt of a new society but recoiled from political activism; he was an atheist enthralled by the possibility of transcendent experiences.

Paradox was a hallmark of his theories as well as his life. Self-actualized people, Maslow told us, transcend dichotomies and resolve oppositions. They are not entirely this nor that, and they realize the world isn't either. Thus, it seemed appropriate to me when, in college, I first drank in Maslow's books, to find myself decidedly ambivalent about what he had to say. I wrote papers taking him to task for certain ideas, yet his broader vision for psychology enthralled me and became part of me. With the affective charge having abated somewhat, with a quieter affirmation here and a more muted objection there, I feel much the same way a couple of decades later.

A Closer Look at "Self-Actualization"

The specific characteristics that Maslow attributed to the self-actualized individual seem less important to me than the fact that he paid attention to growing, mature, fully functioning people in the first place. Psychology had hitherto been much more interested in pathology, and when mental health was discussed at all, it was implicitly understood in terms of adaptation to social norms, such that "healthy" and "normal" were re-

Originally published in *Perceiving, Behaving, Becoming: Lessons Learned* in 1999.

garded as interchangeable. Maslow argued that "adjustment is, very definitely, *not* necessarily synonymous with psychological health" (Maslow 1968, p. 212). (Thus, confronted with "proof" that an instructional technique, or discipline system, in the classroom is effective, we might well ask, "Effective at what?"—knowing that the answer may have more to do with adaptation and adjustment, with the perpetuation of the status quo, than with genuine health.) In addition to challenging the view of health as adaptation, Maslow (along with Marie Jahoda, Erich Fromm, and other humanists) also took issue with the medical model's view of health as tantamount to the absence of illness, insisting instead on a *positive* definition of health—one that specified what human beings are like at their best.

The call for psychologists to investigate health was not a dispassionate recommendation for Maslow, analogous to asking that more attention be paid to this or that developmental stage. Rather, it reflected a belief that there was much about us humans that *was* healthy, admirable, worth celebrating. This conviction, shared by Carl Rogers and others, has provided a contemporary counterpoint to the bleak view of our species offered by Freud, Hobbes, and the doctrine of Original Sin. I found the humanists' benign perspective refreshing when I first encountered it, and I subsequently discovered a cache of empirical evidence that, to some extent at least, corroborated what Maslow and others had been saying (Kohn 1990). More recently, I have become interested in exposing and criticizing the cynical assumptions about children that underlie mainstream arguments for classroom management (Kohn 1996, chap. 1) and character education (Kohn 1997).

Still, I have my reservations. In good Maslovian form, I wonder whether Humans as Good is just the mirror image of Humans as Bad, equally reductive and ultimately as unconvincing.

But what is the alternative position? That we are somewhere in between? Maybe. That we are both good and evil? If this is closer to the truth, it suggests that we must come to terms with a full range of human impulses and capacities, as has been argued by Rollo May (1982), perhaps the most incisive and complicated thinker associated with humanistic psychology. Ultimately, though, the alternative to Good vs. Evil may be not that we are both, but that we are neither—at least if good and evil are construed as givens.

The existentialist tradition, which May (1958) single-handedly introduced to American psychology, calls into question the idea of a fixed human nature, emphasizing instead how much we determine our own nature and, more to the point, how we decide not just *whether* to be good but what it *means* to call something "good" in the first place. Both who we are and how we should act are more within the realm of human choice than we sometimes care to acknowledge. Biological determinism is therefore no less problematic just because we attribute agreeable qualities (e.g., altruism, the capacity to be self-actualizing) rather than disagreeable qualities (e.g., aggression, selfishness) to our essential makeup. The former characteristics may be nice, but that does not make it any less problematic to think of them as "natural" if, in fact, we are creators as much as discoverers, composers as much as archaeologists.

Maslow (1968, p. 193) gave some credence to this idea, but the bulk of his life's work was informed by precisely the opposite conviction. Healthy people, he believed, are those who actualize—that is, make real—what they already are. He spoke frequently of an "inner nature" and saw psychotherapy as an attempt to help "the person to *discover* his Identity, his Real Self, in a word, his own subjective biology, which he can *then* proceed to actualize, to 'make himself,' to 'choose' " (1976, p. 179).

Among the problems with this position is that it commits what philosophers since Hume have identified as the "naturalistic fallacy," which refers to the attempt to derive a value from a fact. Just agreeing that something is part of human nature—or, for that matter, that it is true to *my* nature—does not in and of itself permit us to say that this thing is desirable, good, or healthy. Thus, Maslow (1968, p. 205) was guilty of a very basic conceptual error when he declared that "the word *ought* need not be used" and we can rely on "a naturalistic system of values, a by-product of the empirical description of the deepest tendencies of the human species and of specific individuals." In another essay, he stated that "the best way for a person to discover what he ought to do is to find out who and what he is, because the path to ethical and value decisions, to wiser choices, to oughtness, is via 'isness' . . . Many problems simply disappear; many others are easily solved by knowing what is in conformity with one's nature, what is suitable and right" (1976, pp. 106–7).

In fact, the problems—and the necessity of demonstrating why something is good or ought to be done—do not disappear at all. They are just conveniently avoided when we blithely invite people to "find their inner selves."

Look at it this way: If Maslow says it is good to be who we really are, that statement is offered either as an analytic truth or an empirical truth. If it's analytical, he is basically saying it is true by definition, that "in conformity with one's nature" is part of the *meaning* of words like "right" or "healthy." This requires some justification; one can't, after all, prove a contention just by defining it to be true. If his claim is empirical, though, then he is suggesting that science can show that people do in fact move toward health or goodness (given certain facilitating environmental conditions), or that what is in conformity with one's nature does in fact turn out to be healthy. In this case, Maslow obviously has some independent standard of what constitutes health or goodness, some value by which our actions can be judged. M. Brewster Smith, a critic from within humanistic psychology, saw the latter as the only way to read Maslow: "His empirical definition of psychological health or self-actualization thus rests, at root, on his own implicit values that underlie this global judgment. The array of characteristics that he reports must then be regarded not as an empirical description of the fully human . . . but rather as an explication of his implicit conception of the fully human, of his orienting frame of human values . . . I like them, but that is beside the point" (Smith 1973, p. 24).

Of course, there is nothing wrong with making value judgments about what humans ought to be like—only with pretending after the fact that they are not really value judgments at all but are magically contained within factual statements about what we *are* like.

Then there is the painfully obvious question: How can we defend the "natural" tendencies of a species that commits unspeakable atrocities with some regularity? The humanists' only move here is to discount the bad stuff as not reflective of our *deepest* tendencies, as not being in tune with our *real* nature. But how do we know what is deepest or most real? Have we, once again, simply defined anything evil as less deep or true than the good? How can such a decision be defended? The humanists offer a key caveat, of course, which is that health consists of what people freely choose "under certain conditions that we have learned to call good"; the choices that reveal our nature are those made by "sound adults or children who are not yet twisted and distorted" (Maslow 1970, pp. 272, 278). But these value-laden qualifiers undermine any claim that we can skip the oughts and proceed directly from facts to values[1]; they essentially prove Smith (1973, p. 25) correct when he concludes that "our biology cannot be made to carry our ethics as Maslow would have it."

Needs

If the specifics of Maslow's definition of health become more problematic upon closer inspection, his willingness to devote serious attention to the subject may be his more admirable, and lasting, legacy. Exactly the same is true of his contribution to the study of what people need. Maslow proposed that the extent to which our needs are met can predict how well we function, and this insight helps us understand what happens in families, classrooms, workplaces, and society more generally. Particularly with respect to children, we can predict that more developmentally appropriate and constructive practices will follow when our first question is "What do kids need, and how can we meet those needs?" as opposed to "How can we get kids to do what we tell them?" Any number of thinkers have made a similar point—one thinks of the motivational psychologists Edward Deci and Richard Ryan or the psychiatrist William Glasser, for example— but back in the 1940s Maslow helped all of us to grasp the importance of ensuring, as he later put it, "that the child's basic psychological needs are satisfied" (1976, p. 183).

Maslow explicitly repudiated the homeostatic (or tension-reduction) view that says we, like all organisms, are motivated chiefly to satisfy our inborn needs in an effort to return to a condition of rest or stasis. Maslow (1968, p. 30) believed that "gratification of one need and its consequent removal from the center of the stage brings about not a state of rest . . . but rather the emergence into consciousness of another 'higher' need." The higher needs are distinguished, among other things, by seeming more like desires than compulsions.

This proposition simultaneously challenges the Freudian model, which is essentially homeostatic, and the behaviorist model, which sees us as no more than "repertoires of behaviors" that are, in turn, fully determined by "environmental contingencies." The humanistic view holds that we are not at the mercy of outside forces; our motivations often come from within and, moreover, have a freely chosen component to them. ("The self-actualizer's wishes and plans are the primary determiners, rather than stresses from the environment" [1968, p. 35].) The goal is not stasis but continual growth, not a respite from needs but a shift to different kinds of needs and more joy in satisfying them.

Maslow (1968, pp. 202–3) distinguished between deficiency and growth motivation, between need-interested and need-disinterested perception, and between D (for Deficiency) love and B (for Being) love. I have found this set of distinctions both provocative and useful in thinking about a range of issues, notwithstanding the inherent limitations of dualities. Truly, some people see what they need to see, while others are more successful at encountering a new idea or situation without construing it as a means to their own ends, without filtering it through their own emotional hurts and histories. Some people attach themselves to others with a desperation suggesting D-love, much as a starving person would approach a plate of food, while others have the emotional freedom to appreciate others for who they are, feeling more flexible and autonomous, less driven and less likely to turn others into something they aren't. The same basic distinction can be applied to how one approaches ideas—a purer B-cognition presumably being one goal of education—or even to one's sense of humor. Consistent with the B vs. D formulation, for example, one might argue that competitiveness is properly understood as a deficiency-motivated trait: Being good at an activity may be something we choose to do, but winning is experienced as something we *have* to do, psychologically speaking (Kohn 1986, p. 101). Tragically, competition exacerbates rather than satisfies that lower-level need.

Again, though, the ambivalence: While making use of Maslow's framework, I have found myself wincing at its epistemological implications. The very idea of "need-free perception," suggesting that healthy individuals can see things (and people) as they really are, derives from Maslow's (1968, p. 201) straight-faced talk about "the world of unyielding facts." It is also a correlative of his assertion that it is possible for psychologists to study our "inner nature scientifically and objectively (that is, with the right kind of 'science') and to discover what it is like (*discover*—not invent or construct)" (1968, p. 191). This brand of naive, even quaint, empiricism has been rudely displaced by twentieth-century physics, to say nothing of modern constructivism. No matter how healthy we may be, "knowledge does not reflect an 'objective' ontological reality, but exclusively an ordering and organization of a world constituted by our experience" (von Glaserfeld 1984, p. 24). Progressive educators may be attracted both to Maslow's humanism and to a constructivist understanding of learning, but it is important to acknowledge that the two cannot be entirely reconciled.

Where Maslow gets into more trouble is where his theory gets more specific (and more famous): the well-known triangle on which needs are arrayed. Here the two-stage hierarchy of needs—deficiency and growth—is supplanted by a five-stage hierarchy, as follows: At the bottom are physiological needs, which are "prepotent," meaning that they must be satisfied first. When people get food and other bodily necessities, they are then concerned about safety. After safety comes the need for belongingness or love, then esteem or achievement, and finally, at the top of the triangle, comes the need for self-actualization, which he defined as "the desire to become more and more what one idiosyncratically is, to become everything that one is capable of becoming" (Maslow 1970, p. 46). (Incidentally, in the revised edition to his basic text on motivation, published the year he died, Maslow made it clear that he believed "self-actualization does not occur in young people" [p. xx].)

Before mentioning some problems with the hierarchy of needs, we should take a moment to clear up a confusion that is not Maslow's fault. Some people, casually invoking his theory, declare that it is appropriate and even necessary to provide extrinsic inducements (notably, rewards) to an individual, because only later will he or she be ready to "move up" to the level of intrinsic motivation. This formulation is based on several errors. First, it assumes that because intrinsic motivation is desirable, it must be a higher need in the sense that it appears at a later stage of development. In fact, however, Maslow's entire theory of motivation and the whole range of needs it embraces (including the need for self-actualization) could be said to be intrinsic, or part of who we are. We do not always find ourselves in environments that meet these needs and fulfill our potential, but intrinsic motivation, seen as a function of these needs, is present from the start.

What is not there from the start, however, is an extrinsic orientation. There is a profound difference between the things we need (e.g., food, money, approval) and the deliberate use of these things *as rewards* to induce people to behave in a certain way. Those who are controlled with rewards may well come to lose interest in what they have been rewarded for doing (Kohn 1993) and thereafter may seem extrinsically oriented. But this does not mean that a dependence on (or an expectation of) extrinsic rewards is prepotent over intrinsic, in Maslow's language. In fact, one study of nearly eight hundred employed adults found "no evidence that workers must learn to appreciate or need intrinsic satisfaction . . . Extrinsic rewards become an important determinant of overall job satisfaction only among workers for whom intrinsic rewards are relatively unavailable" (Gruenberg 1980, p. 268). The same may be said of students who appear to be dependent on extrinsic rewards such as grades, stickers, pizza, and praise: What they really needed from the beginning simply wasn't available.

The concept of intrinsic motivation is generally traced back to the work of Robert White (on competence), Richard deCharms (on self-determination), and finally to Harry Harlow, who was apparently the first to use the term in 1950. Maslow, interestingly, was Harlow's first doctoral student some two decades before Harlow and his colleagues discovered that rhesus monkeys not only learned how to operate a mechanical puzzle in the absence of food rewards, but that the introduction of rewards "seriously disrupted the efficient puzzle solution which they had repeatedly demonstrated previously" (Harlow et al. 1950, p. 231). Maslow's name does not appear prominently in most accounts of intrinsic motivation, but there is no doubt that his personality theory helped set the stage for an understanding of the concept. For what it's worth, I'm certain that my own interest in the topic was indirectly an outgrowth of my immersion in Maslow's work some time earlier.

Let us stipulate, then, that intrinsic motivation is part of Maslow's legacy and that misunderstandings of the "need" for extrinsic motivators are not his fault. Nevertheless, there are real problems with his hierarchy of needs, beginning with the slipperiness of his terms and the difficulty of demonstrating empirically whether or not he was right. It is not just that Maslow was "out ahead of the data," as he himself put it, but that it is virtually impossible to test his theory:

For example, what behavior should or should not be included in each need category? How can a need be gratified out of existence? What does dominance of a given need mean? What are the conditions under which the theory is operative? How does the shift from one need to another take place? Do people also go down the hierarchy as they go up in it? Is there an independent hierarchy for each situation or do people develop a general hierarchy for all situations? What is the time span for the unfolding of the hierarchy? These and similar questions are not answered by Maslow and are open for many interpretations. The most problematic aspect of Maslow's theory, however, is that . . . it is not clear what is meant by the concept of need (Wahba and Bridwell 1976, p. 234).

To the extent one *can* meaningfully derive testable hypotheses from Maslow's theory, moreover, there is serious reason to think it was wrong. First, the underlying assumption is remarkably deterministic, and one could argue that "what we choose to do depends more on our ethics than on satisfying needs" (Maccoby 1988, p. 32). If our actions are not in fact driven by a progressive unfolding of inborn needs, then the accuracy—or at least the functional relevance—of the theory is called into question. Second, while it may be intuitively plausible to talk about safety needs, belongingness needs, and so on, "there is no clear evidence that human needs are classified in five distinct categories, or that these categories are structured in a special hierarchy" (Wahba and Bridwell 1976, p. 224). In fact, there is some evidence to the contrary. Finally, it has never been shown that one need triggers the next in the way Maslow described. If he was right, the satisfaction of a given need—accepting for the sake of the argument that a need can ever really be "satisfied"—should cause that need to subside and also cause the next need in the hierarchy to become more salient. Attempts to demonstrate this, however, have generally failed (e.g., Hall and Nougaim 1968, Lawler and Suttle 1972).

The subjects in much of the research on this topic have been corporate managers, possibly limiting the generalizability of the negative findings; what's more, the studies have been plagued by a number of methodological limitations (see Wicker et al. 1993). But even the data that do appear to be supportive may not rescue the theory as a whole. It can be shown that people think less about food once they are fed, but that doesn't demonstrate that the same principle operates with higher needs. It can be shown that corporate employees start out being preoccupied with safety needs and later become more concerned about achievement, but this may be a function of changing social roles or situations rather than proof of some inherent relationship among innate needs that plays out automatically.

Once the empirical basis for Maslow's hierarchy has been challenged, one is free to identify and question the values that led him to arrange these needs in the order he did. That Maslow seems to regard the need for love or affiliation as "lower" than the need for self-actualization or even achievement seems to suggest that the desire to connect with others is "some sort of irritant that needs fixing so that people will be free to focus on more important things such as achievement and success" (Sergiovanni 1994, pp. 65–66). One has difficulty imagining this particular hierarchy being proposed by a female or Asian psychologist, for example.

Maslow has been faulted for "an atomistic view of the self" (Geller 1982, p. 69), for his premise that we "achieve full human-ness through an intense affair with the self" (Aron 1986, p. 99).[2]

But even those who are sympathetic to the individualism that undergirds his writings, including his equation of health with *self*-actualization, ought to keep in mind that this is the world-view of a particular historical period and a particular set of cultural assumptions. Maslow was sufficiently schooled in anthropology (and sufficiently influenced by Ruth Benedict) to be cautious about explicitly claiming his observations were universal truths (e.g., see Maslow 1970, pp. 54–55), yet much of his work is presented as being a description of human nature. Anyone enamored of self-actualization theory would do well to remember what Clifford Geertz observed: "The Western conception of the person as a bounded, unique, more or less integrated motivational and cognitive universe, a dynamic center of awareness, emotion, judgment, and action organized into a distinctive whole and set contrastively against both other such wholes and against its social and natural background, is, however incorrigible it may seem to us, a rather peculiar idea within the context of the world's cultures" (Geertz 1983, p. 59).

Maslow on Education

Maslow had remarkably little to say on the subject of education. He offered little evidence of careful thought about pedagogical matters even in an article he wrote for the *Harvard Educational Review* (reprinted in Maslow 1976, chap. 13). His few paragraphs on the subject consisted of a call for education to foster "growth toward self-actualization" (1968, p. 212), "learning of the heart" (1970, p. 282), "learning who you are," "being able to hear your inner voices" (1976, p. 177), and for education to "refreshen consciousness so that we are continually aware of the beauty and wonder of life" (1976, p. 183). He thought there should be more emphasis on creativity and developing a "healthy unconscious" (1968, p. 208), and more concern, at least in our culture, with "spontaneity, the ability to be expressive, passive, unwilled..." (1968, p. 198). By contrast, schools were said to place too much emphasis on "purely abstract thinking" (1968, p. 208) and "implanting the greatest number of facts into the greatest possible number of children" (1976, p. 173).

When asked about education, Maslow tended to think primarily about the college years—understandably, since he spent most of his life in universities. He was dismayed at the prevailing preoccupation with "means, i.e., grades, degrees, credits, diplomas, rather than with ends, i.e., wisdom, understanding, good judgment, good taste" (1970, p. 282). He wrote about students so driven by "extrinsic rewards" that they could not fathom why anyone would read a book that wasn't required for a course, and he remarked that learning itself was so little valued that "leaving college before the completion of one's senior year is considered to be a waste of time by the society and a minor tragedy by parents" (1976, pp. 174–75). By way of contrast, he told a story about Upton Sinclair: "When Sinclair was a young man, he found that he was unable to raise the tuition money needed to attend college. Upon careful reading of the college catalogue, however, he found that if a student failed a course, he received no credit for the course, but was obliged to take another course in its place. The college did not charge the student for the second course, reasoning that he had already paid once for his credit. Sinclair took advantage of this policy and got a free education by deliberately failing all his courses" (1976, pp. 174–75).

The little that he did write on education, per se, will likely continue to elicit enthusiasm among progressives and derision among traditionalists. To be sure, Maslow's message is not well suited to an era that seems ever more determined to judge its schools on the basis of standardized-test scores and that ratchets up standards to make students more "competitive." But even those of us who nod at Maslow's remarks about extrinsic rewards (and smile at the Sinclair anecdote) may be forgiven for finding all the earnest talk about spontaneity and inner voices to be rather less than helpful. Authenticity never goes out of date, but Maslow's declarations are sometimes so sweeping and simplistic as to provoke a twinge of embarrassment, as, for example, when he informs educators that addicts "will give up drugs easily if you offer them instead some meaning to their lives" (1976, p. 180) or that even when "parents convey their own distorted patterns of behavior to the child . . . if the teacher's are healthier and stronger, the children will imitate these instead" (p. 181).

There is very little of substance or specificity in Maslow's writings to guide teachers through the exigencies of life in real classrooms. Only once that I am aware of did he even acknowledge the structural barriers that might constrain teachers from encouraging peak experiences in their students.[3] In general, while Maslow's thoughts about psychology may be indirectly relevant to education, just as they may be indirectly relevant to architecture or any other field, he was clearly not steeped in the particulars of life at school or how children learn.

On the other hand, educators absorb and reflect a set of assumptions about who we are as human beings and what we can (and ought to) become. Maslow's optimism, his tireless attention to growth and health, and his analysis of motivation and needs collectively define a psychological perspective that is richer, deeper, and more heuristic than the behaviorism that captivated Maslow himself at age twenty but which he later transcended. We might take issue with any number of his ideas while still finding his conception of human potential a basis for lively discussion and a source of energy and inspiration.

Notes

1. I believe these objections also apply to Lawrence Kohlberg's (1971) cleverer and more self-conscious attempt to do essentially the same thing with his stage theory of moral development.

2. Aron's essay is reprinted in *Politics and Innocence*, a fascinating collection devoted to the social and political implications of humanistic psychology. Contributions by Walter Nord and Allan R. Buss, in particular, explore the conservative and individualistic implications of humanistic psychology and especially of Maslow's work. As Buss (1986, p. 140) puts it, "A theory that disposes one to focus more upon individual freedom and development rather than the larger social reality, works in favor of maintaining that social reality."

3. "Of course, with the traditional model of thirty-five children in one classroom and a curriculum of subject matter which has to be gotten through in a given period of time, the teacher is forced to pay more attention to orderliness and lack of noise than [to] making learning a joyful experience" (Maslow 1976, p. 181).

References

Aron, A. 1986. "Maslow's Other Child." Originally published 1977. Reprinted in *Politics and Innocence: A Humanistic Debate*. Dallas: Saybrook.

Buss, A. 1986. "Humanistic Psychology as Liberal Ideology: The Socio-Historical Roots of Maslow's Theory of Self-Actualization." Originally published 1979. Reprinted in *Politics and Innocence: A Humanistic Debate*. Dallas: Saybrook.

Geertz, C. 1983. "From the Native's Point of View." In *Local Knowledge*. New York: Basic Books.

Geller, L. 1982. "The Failure of Self-Actualization Theory: A Critique of Carl Rogers and Abraham Maslow." *Journal of Humanistic Psychology* 22, no. 2: 56–73.

Gruenberg, B. 1980. "The Happy Worker: An Analysis of Educational and Occupational Differences in Determinants of Job Satisfaction." *American Journal of Sociology* 86: 247–71.

Hall, D. T., and K. E. Nougaim. 1968. "An Examination of Maslow's Need Hierarchy in an Organizational Setting." *Organizational Behavior and Human Performance* 3: 12–35.

Harlow, H. F., M. K. Harlow, and D. R. Meyer. 1950. "Learning Motivated by a Manipulation Drive." *Journal of Experimental Psychology* 40: 228–34.

Hoffman, E. 1988. *The Right to Be Human: A Biography of Abraham Maslow*. Los Angeles: Jeremy P. Tarcher.

Kohlberg, L. 1971. "From *Is* to *Ought*: How to Commit the Naturalistic Fallacy and Get Away with It in the Study of Moral Development." In T. Mischel, ed., *Cognitive Development and Epistemology*. New York: Academic Press.

Kohn, A. 1986. *No Contest: The Case Against Competition*. Boston: Houghton Mifflin.

Kohn, A. 1990. *The Brighter Side of Human Nature: Altruism and Empathy in Everyday Life*. New York: Basic Books.

Kohn, A. 1993. *Punished by Rewards: The Trouble with Gold Stars, Incentive Plans, A's, Praise, and Other Bribes*. Boston: Houghton Mifflin.

Kohn, A. 1996. *Beyond Discipline: From Compliance to Community*. Alexandria, Va.: ASCD.

Kohn, A. 1997. "How Not to Teach Values: A Critical Look at Character Education." *Phi Delta Kappan* (February): 429–39.

Lawler, E. E. III, and J. L. Suttle. 1972. "A Causal Correlational Test of the Need Hierarchy Concept." *Organizational Behavior and Human Performance* 7: 265–87.

Maccoby, M. 1988. *Why Work: Leading the New Generation*. New York: Simon and Schuster.

Maslow, A. H. 1968. *Toward a Psychology of Being*. 2nd ed. New York: D. Van Nostrand.

Maslow, A. H. 1970. *Motivation and Personality*. 2nd ed. New York: Harper & Row.

Maslow, A. H. 1976. *The Farther Reaches of Human Nature*. New York: Penguin.

May, R. 1958. "The Origins and Significance of the Existential Movement in Psychology" and "Contributions of Existential Psychotherapy." In R. May, E. Angel, and H. F. Ellenberger, eds., *Existence: A New Dimension in Psychiatry and Psychology*. New York: Touchstone.

May, R. 1982. "The Problem of Evil: An Open Letter to Carl Rogers." *Journal of Humanistic Psychology* 22 (Summer): 10–21.

Sergiovanni, T. 1994. *Building Community in Schools*. San Francisco: Jossey-Bass.

Smith, M. B. 1973. "On Self-Actualization." *Journal of Humanistic Psychology* 13, no. 2: 17–33.

von Glaserfeld, E. 1984. "An Introduction to Radical Constructivism." In P. Watzlawick, ed., *The Invented Reality*. New York: Norton.

Wahba, M. A., and L. G. Bridwell. 1976. "Maslow Reconsidered: A Review of Research on the Need Hierarchy Theory." *Organizational Behavior and Human Performance* 15: 212–40.

Wicker, F. W., G. Brown, J. A. Wiehe, A. S. Hagen, and J. L. Reed. 1993. "On Reconsidering Maslow: An Examination of the Deprivation/Domination Proposition." *Journal of Research in Personality* 27: 118–33.

Five: School Reform and the Study of Education

15. Almost There, But Not Quite

The late educational researcher John Nicholls once remarked to me that he had met a lot of administrators who "don't want to hear a buzz of excitement in classrooms—they want to hear nothing." His implication was that some teachers strive to keep tight control over students less because of their principles than because of their principals. After all, their evaluations may depend not on whether their students are engaged and happy, or curious and caring, but rather on whether they are silent and orderly.

Schools can still purchase standardized discipline programs—or, for that matter, develop home-grown strategies—that rely on heavy-handed, old-school techniques intended to break down students' resistance and coerce them into conformity. These days, though, programs more commonly use progressive rhetoric and palatable-sounding strategies. They may invoke such notions as dignity, cooperation, responsibility, love, and logic. They may rely on positive reinforcement rather than punishment, and use softer words to describe the latter. In fact, they may appear so reassuringly humanistic that we have to remind ourselves the basic objective—compliance—is unchanged.

Rudolf Dreikurs, for example, is an author I liked a lot . . . until I finally sat down and read him. The "logical consequences" programs that he inspired, as well as other attempts to use pleasant-sounding means to achieve authoritarian ends, prompted me to write a book on the subject a few years back (Kohn 1996). More recently, a group of researchers confirmed that, although most teachers try to maintain "control with a light touch," their goal typically remains to control students. Almost all the teachers interviewed by the researchers endorsed the need to teach

Originally published in *Educational Leadership* in 2003.

"good citizenship," but it turned out that most defined this in terms of "maintaining order and work effort . . . following rules [or] respecting authority" (Brint et al. 2001, pp. 173, 175).

Asking the Right Questions

What matters, then, are the fundamental questions that drive educational practice, even if they are not posed explicitly. Some teachers and administrators want to know, How can we get these kids to obey? What practical techniques can you offer that will cause students to show up, sit down, and do what they're told? But other educators begin from an entirely different point of departure. They ask, What do these kids need—and how can we meet those needs?

The more I visit classrooms, talk with teachers, and read the literature, the more convinced I become that you can predict what a school will look like and feel like just from knowing which set of questions the adults care about more. You don't even need to know the answers they've found (which tactics they will use to secure compliance, in the first case; what they believe children need, in the second). The questions are what matter.

Even educators who try to focus on students' needs, however, may feel themselves caught in an undertow, pulled back to traditional assumptions and practices that result in doing things *to* students rather than working *with* them. Some aren't even aware that this is happening. I have long been intrigued by the tendency to assume one has arrived when, in fact, there is still a lot further to go. Consultants will tell you that few barriers to change are as intractable as the belief that one doesn't need to change. When you tell some teachers about a new approach, they instantly respond, "Oh, I'm already doing that." And sometimes they are— sort of, but not entirely.

In a classic essay, David K. Cohen described a math teacher

who firmly believed she was teaching for understanding. Indeed, she was using many innovative activities and materials—for example, having her students do number sentences and calendar activities—yet she had adopted them without questioning her traditional assumptions about pedagogy, such as the idea that the goal is to produce right answers rather than to understand mathematical principles from the inside out. The result was a classroom that subtly discouraged students from exploring ideas, even as the teacher prided herself on how effectively she encouraged such exploration (Cohen, 1990; also see Campbell 1996).

Going Part of the Way

Exactly the same partial success, often accompanied by a gap between perception and reality, shows up in the way many classrooms are structured, how they feel to students, how people are treated. A half-dozen examples follow. You may find yourself adding more.

1. Blaming the Students: Some teachers consciously try to create a "working with" classroom, yet automatically assume that when students act inappropriately, they have a behavior problem that must be fixed. It is the students who must change, and the teacher stands by to help them do so.

Norman Kunc (n.d.), who conducts workshops on inclusive education and noncoercive practices, points out that "what we call 'behavior problems' are often situations of legitimate conflict; we just get to call them behavior problems because we have more power" than the students do. (You're not allowed to say that your spouse has a behavior problem.) Some teachers respond with fury when they have a conflict with a student, and some respond with understanding, but few teachers have the courage to reflect on how they may need to reconsider their own decisions. A San Diego educator, Donna Marriott, stands out for having done just that: "If a child starts to act up, I have learned to ask myself: 'How have I failed this child? What is it about this lesson that is leaving her outside the learning? How can I adapt my plan to engage this child?' I stopped blaming my children" (2001, p. 27).

Unsettling as it may be to acknowledge, an awful lot of smart, warm, empathic teachers continue to blame their children when things go wrong—and they may not even be aware that they are doing this.

2. Keeping Control of the Classroom: It is possible to allow students to make decisions in the classroom—even boast about how they are empowered—while limiting the number, significance, or impact of these choices to ensure that the teacher remains comfortably in control. One can hold class meetings, for example, but unilaterally determine what will be discussed, who will speak and when, how long the meeting will last, and so on. Or consider a teacher in Washington state who boldly hung a sign at the front of her classroom that read "Think for yourself; the teacher might be wrong!" Only gradually did she begin to realize that her classroom remained in important ways teacher-centered rather than learner-centered. Her practices were still "authoritarian," as she later realized: "I wanted [students] to think for themselves, but only so long as their thinking didn't slow down my predetermined lesson plan or get in the way of my teacher-led activity or argue against my classroom policies" (Coe 1997, p. 7; also see Miranda 1999).

3. Missing the Systemic Factors: Some educators work hard to cultivate a caring relationship with each student, to earn his or her respect and trust. They understand how traditional management techniques erode those relationships. However, problems persist in their classrooms, at least partly because the teachers lack a wider perspective that illuminates what is happening among the individuals involved. As Sylwester (2000, p. 23) writes, "Misbehavior is to a classroom what pain is to a body—a useful status report that something isn't working as it should." The underlying problem of which that misbehavior is but a symptom may not be limited to the needs of a given child. Just as some therapists move beyond the "identified patient" to consider the dynamics of the family as a whole, the teacher may need to address at the systemic level his or her own role and the way all the students in the classroom interact.

Many teachers believe that everything would be perfect if only they could get rid of a particular student who is always causing trouble. But if that student is finally removed, another one may pop up, like the next tissue in the box, to fill the role previously played by his classmate. In other words, educators can make only so much progress if they understand individuals but overlook roles and systems.

4. Ignoring Problems with the Curriculum: Teachers who work with students to create a caring community—and who respond constructively to setbacks that develop—sometimes pay insufficient attention to deficiencies in the academic curriculum. As a result, they are forever struggling to get students to pay attention to tasks that, frankly, don't deserve their attention. Misbehavior may continue primarily because students resist instruction that emphasizes decontextualized skills or requires rote recall, activities intended to raise test scores rather than to answer authentic questions, lessons that they find neither relevant nor engaging—and that they had little or no role in designing. Truly, the question of how a classroom is "managed" is inextricably linked to the theory of learning that informs curriculum content and instruction. This is why I have talked, only half in jest, about a modest attempt to overthrow the entire field of classroom management. No matter how much progress is made in that field, it can never accomplish meaningful goals if it is divorced from pedagogical matters.

5. Settling for Self-Discipline: Some educators reject rewards and punishments, believing, as I do, that a child may come to act in the desired way only in order to receive the former or avoid the latter. They want students to be self-disciplined, to internalize good values so that outside inducements are no longer necessary.

But even this goal is not ambitious enough. The self-disciplined student may not be an autonomous decision maker if the values have been established and imposed from outside, by the adult. Accepting someone else's expectations is very different from developing one's own (and fashioning reasons for them). Creating a classroom whose objective is for students to internalize good behavior or good values begs the question of what is meant by "good." Moreover, it may amount to trying to direct students by remote control.

6. Manipulating with "Positive Reinforcement": Finally, educators who resist the usual carrot-and-stick approach to discipline may fail to understand that praise is just another carrot—that is, an extrinsic inducement—analogous to a sticker, an A, a pizza, or a dollar. Even classrooms that otherwise seem inviting are often marred by eruptions of evaluation from the teacher, as students are told they've done a "good job." In these classrooms, support and approval are made contingent on doing what pleases or impresses the teacher—precisely the opposite of the unconditional acceptance and empowerment that children need.

Considerable evidence (reviewed in Kohn 1993, chap. 6) demonstrates that positive reinforcement tends to make children more dependent on adult approval and less interested in whatever they had to do to get that approval—for example, learning or helping. This problem is not limited to praise that is excessive, effusive, or transparently manipulative. Rather, the whole idea of offering a verbal reward to encourage a particular behavior is an example of "doing to" rather than "working with." Because many wonderful teachers have never been invited to consider this possibility, they may be taking away with one hand what they work so hard to offer with the other.

Going Further

None of these six problems is necessarily fatal. Teachers who feel a twinge of guilty recognition while reading about them may well have classrooms that, in most respects, provide successful and even inspiring learning environments. One hopes that the people who made them that way are willing to challenge not only the conventional wisdom (for example, about the nature of children or the need for discipline) but also their own practices and premises. We ought to be pleased with how far we've come—but not so pleased that we can't see how much further there is to go.

References

Brint, S., M. F. Contreras, and M. T. Matthews. 2001. "Socialization Messages in Primary Schools: An Organizational Analysis." *Sociology of Education* 74: 157–80.

Campbell, P. F. 1996. "Empowering Children and Teachers in the Elementary Mathematics Classrooms of Urban Schools." *Urban Education* 30, no. 4: 449–75.

Coe, C. 1997. "Turning Over Classroom Decision Making: A Teacher's Experience Over Time." *The Active Learner: A Foxfire Journal for Teachers* (August): 7–9, 38.

Cohen, D. K. 1990. "A Revolution in One Classroom: The Case of Mrs. Oublier." *Educational Evaluation and Policy Analysis* 12, no. 3: 311–29.

Kohn, A. 1993. *Punished by Rewards.* Boston: Houghton Mifflin.

Kohn, A. 1996. *Beyond Discipline: From Compliance to Community.* Alexandria, Va.: ASCD.

Kunc, N. (n.d.) "Presentation Descriptions for Human Services." (Online.) Available at www.normemma.com/hmsvouts.htm.

Marriott, D. M. 2001. "At-Risk Learners—An Insider's Perspective." *Education Week* (February 21): 25, 27.

Miranda, S. 1999. "Yours, Mine, or Ours?" *Rethinking Schools* 13, no.4 (Summer): 10–11.

Sylwester, R. 2000. "Unconscious Emotions, Conscious Feelings." *Educational Leadership* 58, no. 3 (November): 20–24.

16. Education's Rotten Apples

Like other people, educators often hold theories about how the world works, or how one ought to act, that are never named, never checked for accuracy, never even consciously recognized. One of the most popular of these theories is a very appealing blend of pragmatism and relativism that might be called "the more, the merrier." People subscribing to this view tend to dismiss arguments that a given educational practice is bad news and ought to be replaced by another. "Why not do both?" they ask. "No reason to throw anything out of your toolbox. Use everything that works."

But what if something that works to accomplish one goal ends up impeding another? And what if two very different strategies are inversely related, such that they work at cross purposes? As it happens, converging evidence from different educational arenas tends to support exactly these concerns. Particularly when practices that might be called, for lack of better labels, progressive and traditional are used at the same time, the latter often has the effect of undermining the former.

Example 1 comes from the world of math instruction. A few years back, a researcher named Michelle Perry published a study in the journal *Cognitive Development* that looked at different ways of teaching children the concept of equivalence, as expressed in problems such as $4 + 6 + 9 = \underline{} + 9$. Fourth- and fifth-graders, none of whom knew how to solve such problems, were divided into two groups. Some were taught the underlying principle ("The goal of a problem like this is to find . . ."), while others were given step-by-step instructions ("Add up all the numbers on the left side, and then subtract the number on the right side").

Both approaches were effective at helping students solve

Originally published in *Education Week* in 2002.

problems just like the initial one. Consistent with other research, however, the principle-based approach was much better at helping them transfer their knowledge to a slightly different kind of problem—for example, multiplying and dividing numbers to reach equivalence. Direct instruction of a technique for getting the right answer produced shallow learning.

But why not do both? What if students were taught the procedure *and* the principle? Here's where it gets interesting. Regardless of the order in which these two kinds of instruction were presented, students who were taught both ways didn't do any better on the transfer problems than did those who were taught only the procedure—which means they did far worse than students who were taught only the principle. Teaching for understanding didn't offset the destructive effects of telling them how to get the answer. Any step-by-step instruction in how to solve such problems put learners at a disadvantage; the absence of such instruction was required for them to understand.

Example 2 has to do with how learning is evaluated. In a study that appeared in the *British Journal of Educational Psychology,* Ruth Butler took fifth- and sixth-graders, including both high- and low-achieving students, and asked them to work on some word-construction and creative-thinking tasks. One-third of them then received feedback in narrative form, one-third received grades for their performance, and one-third received both comments and grades.

The first finding: Irrespective of how well they had been doing in school, students were subsequently less successful at the tasks, and also reported less interest in those tasks, if they received a grade rather than narrative feedback. Other research has produced the same result: Grades almost always have a detrimental effect on how well students learn and how interested they are in the topic they're learning.

But because Butler had thought to include a third experimental condition—grades plus comments—she was able to document that the negative effects of grading, on both performance and interest, were not mitigated by the addition of a comment. In fact, with the task that required more original thinking, the students' performance was highest with comments, lower with grades, and lowest of all with both. These differences were all statistically significant, and they applied to high- and low-achieving students alike. As in Michelle Perry's math study, the more traditional practice not only didn't help, but actually wiped out the positive effects of the alternative strategy.

One recalls the bit of folk wisdom—confirmed by generations of farmers and grocers—warning that a rotten apple can spoil a barrel full of good apples. It would be pushing things to postulate a kind of educational ethylene released by traditional classroom practices, analogous to the gas given off by bad fruit. But it does seem that the quest for optimal results may sometimes require us to abandon certain practices rather than simply piling other, better practices on top of them.

In other instances, too, the rotten-apple theory offers a better fit with educational reality than does "the more, the merrier." Consider schools that try to have it both ways: They work *with* students who act inappropriately, perhaps even spending time to promote conflict-resolution strategies—but they still haven't let go of heavy-handed policies that amount to doing things *to* students to get compliance. On the one hand: "We're a caring community, committed to solving problems together." On the other hand: "If you do something that displeases us (the people with the power), we'll make you suffer to teach you a lesson."

What might explain these mixed messages? Sometimes a school is in transition, grasping for something better but still holding on to old-fashioned control until everyone becomes sufficiently confident about the new approach to let go of the old. Sometimes a theory even more optimistic than "the more, the merrier" is at work: an "antidote" model that assumes the bad will be detoxified by the good. I haven't seen any hard data one way or the other on this question, but plenty of anecdotal evidence suggests that some schools wind up taking away with one hand what they've given with the other. A peer-mediation program is nice, but its potential to do good is limited if kids are still subject to detentions, suspensions, rewards for obedience, and so on. As a principal in Connecticut observed, after describing her school's struggle to create a more positive climate, "Our original goals were to control student behavior and build community, but along the way we learned that these are conflicting goals." Only when the "doing to" is gone can the "working with" really begin to make some headway.

That smell of good apples going bad also issues from classrooms that try to combine collaboration and competition—for example, by putting students into groups but then setting the groups against one another. The reason for cooperative learning, students infer, is to defeat another bunch of students learning together. Cooperation becomes merely instrumental, the goal being to triumph over others.

Or consider a teacher who does all the right things to help kids love reading: surrounds them with good books and offers plenty of time to read them; gives kids choices about what to read and how to respond to what they've read; teaches them to read from the beginning through rich stories and other authentic material, with a focus on meaning rather than just on decoding skills. Sometimes, however, those ingredients of literacy are soured by the simultaneous use of reading incentives—either home-grown schemes or slick prefabricated programs (bought with precious book-acquisition funds)—that lead children to regard reading as a tedious prerequisite to receiving points and prizes. It's hard to treat kids like budding bibliophiles when they're also being treated like pets.

Underlying this last example, as well as Ruth Butler's grading study and perhaps even the tension between problem-solving and discipline, is the deeper issue of motivation to learn. Or maybe we should say *motivations* to learn, because the point is that there are qualitatively different kinds. One of psychology's most robust findings is that extrinsic motivation (doing something in order to receive a reward or avoid a punishment) is completely different from—and often inversely related to—intrinsic motivation (doing something for its own sake). The more we offer rewards to "motivate" people, the more they tend to lose interest in whatever they had to do to get the reward.

Some behaviorists have tried to challenge the growing evidence supporting that contention, but the latest major research review—see *Psychological Bulletin,* vol. 125 (1999): 627–68—dispels any lingering doubt about a finding that has by now held up across genders, ages, cultures, settings, and tasks: Two kinds of motivation simply are not better than one. Rather, one (extrinsic) is corrosive of the other (intrinsic)—and intrinsic is the one that counts. To make a difference, therefore, we have to subtract grades, not just add a narrative report. We have to eliminate incentives, not just promote literacy. We have to remove coercive discipline policies, not just build a caring community.

These days, with our attention riveted on the Tougher Standards version of school reform as on a slow-motion train wreck, we may, if we look very carefully, notice another illustration of the rotten-apple phenomenon playing out before our eyes. Top-down demands to raise scores on bad tests are terrible and ought to be vigorously opposed. But what about top-down demands to raise scores on reasonably good tests? What happens when states offer performance-based assessments, but in the context of "accountability" systems—basically, extrinsic pressure—to improve the results?

In a word, the former are destroyed by the latter. Exhibit A is the Kentucky Education Reform Act, rolled out in the early 1990s, which proposed to let students show what they understood rather than just memorizing facts and bubbling in ovals. Unfortunately, their performance triggered a series of rewards and penalties for educators, and schools quickly became pressure cookers. With so much riding on the outcome, technical concerns about reliability came to overshadow pedagogical concerns about improving learning.

Before the decade was out, the best features of the experiment had been dismantled, with conventional tests replacing richer measures. "High-stakes accountability and performance assessment are based on conflicting principles," as Ken Jones and Betty Lou Whitford observed in their summary of the state's reform. "One encourages conformity to externally imposed standards, while the other grows out of emergent interaction between teachers and students."

Exhibit B is the Maryland State Performance Assessment Program, or MSPAP, a system begun around the same time as Kentucky's that has more recently met the same sad fate. It featured open-ended questions and authentic tasks to measure critical thinking, but it, too, was married to high stakes: Schools were publicly ranked, with bonuses for the high scorers and humiliation and threats for the low. Again, the quality of the assessment couldn't protect students and teachers from the toxic effects of what now passes for "accountability": The curriculum was narrowed to focus on MSPAP questions (for example, more structured writing, less creative writing), students had to memorize catchy formulas for producing high-scoring essays, and schools were set against one another in a mutually destructive competition. High-stakes meant high stress for high- and low-performing schools alike.

The death of the MSPAP had other causes, too: relentless opposition from conservatives (whose counterparts in California and Arizona had also succeeded in halting short-lived experiments with authenticity); pressure to chart the results of individual students, rather than sample their performance so as to monitor schools; and concerns about reliability and errors in scoring prompted by lower scores than expected in affluent areas.

These factors aside, though, there are two central lessons to be drawn from Maryland and Kentucky:

1. Even when the assessment is performance-based, teaching to the test is (a) possible, (b) undesirable, and (c) done pervasively (indeed, frantically).

2. Analogous to the economic principle known as Gresham's Law, *bad tests will drive out good tests in a high-stakes environment.* The current accountability fad—which was launched for political, not educational, reasons—inexorably dumbs down assessment. It leaves us with the sort of conventional standardized tests that are more consistent with the purposes of rating and ranking, bribing and threatening.

Then again, we may be witnessing something that transcends the challenges of assessment, a macro-echo of a phenomenon confirmed at the micro-level: The bad stuff has to be eliminated for the good stuff to work.

17. The Folly of Merit Pay

There's no end to the possible uses for that nifty little Latin phrase *Cui bono?*, which means Who benefits? Whose interests are served? It's the right question to ask about a testing regimen guaranteed to make most public schools look as though they're failing. Or about the assumption that people with less power than you have (students, if you're a teacher; teachers, if you're an administrator) are unable to participate in making decisions about what they're going to do every day.

And here's another application: *Cui bono* when we're assured that money is the main reason it's so hard to find good teachers? If only we paid them more, we'd have no trouble attracting and retaining the finest educators that—well, that money can buy. Just accept that premise, and you'll never have to consider the way teachers are treated. In fact, you could continue disrespecting and deskilling them, forcing them to use scripted curriculums and turning them into glorified test-prep technicians. If they seem unhappy, it must be just because they want a bigger paycheck.

In 2000 Public Agenda questioned more than nine hundred new teachers and almost as many college graduates who *didn't* choose a career in education. Its report concluded that, while "teachers do believe that they are underpaid," higher salaries would probably be of limited effectiveness in alleviating teacher shortages because considerations other than money are "significantly more important to most teachers and would-be teachers." Two years later, 44 percent of administrators reported, in another Public Agenda poll, that talented colleagues were being driven out of the field because of "unreasonable standards and accountability."

Meanwhile, a small California survey published in *Phi Delta*

Originally published in *Education Week* in 2003.

Kappan found that the main reason newly credentialed teachers were leaving the profession was not low salaries or difficult children. Rather, those who threw in the towel were most likely to cite what was being done to their schools in the name of "accountability." And the same lesson seems to hold cross-culturally. Mike Baker, a correspondent for BBC News, discovered that an educational "recruitment crisis" exists almost exclusively in those nations "where accountability measures have undermined teachers' autonomy."

That unhappy educators have a lot more on their minds than money shouldn't be surprising in light of half a century of research conducted in other kinds of workplaces. When people are asked what's most important to them, financial concerns show up well behind such factors as interesting work or good people to work with. For example, in a large survey conducted by the Families and Work Institute, "salary/wage" ranked sixteenth on a list of twenty reasons for taking a job. (Interestingly, managers who are asked what *they* believe matters most to their employees tend to mention money—and then proceed to manage on the basis of that error.)

Educational policymakers might be forgiven their short-sightedness if they were just proposing to raise teachers' salaries across the board—or, perhaps, to compensate them appropriately for more responsibilities or for additional training. Instead, though, many are turning to some version of "pay for performance." Here, myopia is complicated by amnesia: For more than a century, such plans have been implemented, then abandoned, then implemented in a different form, then abandoned again. The idea never seems to work, but proponents of merit pay never seem to learn.

Here are educational historians David Tyack and Larry Cuban: "The history of performance-based salary plans has been a merry-go-round. In the main, districts that initially embraced merit pay dropped it after a brief trial." But even "repeated experiences" of failure haven't prevented officials "from proposing merit pay again and again." *Son of Merit Pay: The Sequel* is now playing in Cincinnati, Denver, Minneapolis, New York City, and elsewhere. The leading advocates of this approach—conservatives, economists, and conservative economists—insist that we need only adopt their current incentive schemes and this time teaching really will improve. Honest.

Wade Nelson, a professor at Winona State University, dug up a government commission's evaluation of England's mid-nineteenth-century "payment by results" plan. His summary of that evaluation: Schools became "impoverished learning environments in which nearly total emphasis on performance on the examination left little opportunity for learning." The plan was abandoned.

In *The Public Interest*, a right-wing policy journal, two researchers concluded with apparent disappointment in 1985 that no evidence supported the idea that merit pay "had an appreciable or consistent positive effect on teachers' classroom work." Moreover, they reported that few administrators expected such an effect "even though they had the strongest reason to make such claims."

To this day, enthusiasm for pay for performance runs far ahead of any data supporting its effectiveness—even as measured by standardized test scores, much less by meaningful indicators of learning. But then that, too, echoes the results in other workplaces. To the best of my knowledge, no controlled scientific study has ever found a long-term enhancement of the quality of work as a result of any incentive system. In fact, numerous studies have confirmed that performance on tasks, particularly complex tasks, is generally lower when people are promised a reward for doing them, or for doing them well. As a rule, the more prominent or enticing the reward, the more destructive its effects.

So why are pay-for-performance plans so reliably unsuccessful, if not counterproductive?

1. **Control**. People with more power usually set the goals, establish the criteria, and generally set about trying to change the behavior of those down below. If merit pay feels manipulative and patronizing, that's probably because it is. Moreover, the fact that these programs usually operate at the level of school personnel means, as Maurice Holt pointed out, that the whole enterprise "conveniently moves accountability away from politicians and administrators, who invent and control the system, to those who actually do the work."

2. **Strained relationships**. In its most destructive form, merit pay is set up as a competition, where the point is to best one's colleagues. No wonder just such a proposal, in Norristown, Pennsylvania, was unanimously opposed by teachers and ultimately abandoned. Even those teachers likely to receive a bonus realized that everyone loses—especially the students—when educators are set against one another in a race for artificially scarce rewards.

But pay-for-performance programs don't have to be explicitly competitive in order to undermine collegial relationships. If I end up getting a bonus and you don't, our interactions are likely to be adversely affected, particularly if you think of yourself as a pretty darned good teacher.

Some argue that monetary rewards are less harmful if they're offered to, and made contingent on the performance of, an entire school. But if a school misses out on a bonus, what often ensues is an ugly search for individuals on whom to pin the blame. Also, you can count on seeing less useful collaboration *among* schools, especially if an incentive program is based on their relative standing. Why would one faculty share ideas with another when the goal is to make sure that students in other schools don't do as well as yours? Merit pay based on rankings is about victory, not about excellence. In any case, bribing groups doesn't make any more sense than bribing individuals.

3. Reasons and motives. The premise of merit pay, and indeed of all rewards, is that people *could* be doing a better job but for some reason have decided to wait until it's bribed out of them. This is as insulting as it is inaccurate. Dangling a reward in front of teachers or principals—"Here's what you'll get if things somehow improve"—does nothing to address the complex, systemic factors that are actually responsible for educational deficiencies. Pay for performance is an outgrowth of behaviorism, which is focused on individual organisms, not systems—and, true to its name, looks only at behaviors, not at reasons and motives and the people who have them.

Even if they wouldn't mind larger paychecks, teachers are typically not all that money-driven. They keep telling us in surveys that the magical moment when a student suddenly understands is more important to them than another few bucks. And, as noted above, they're becoming disenchanted these days less because of salary issues than because they don't enjoy being controlled by accountability systems. Equally controlling pay-for-performance plans are based more on neoclassical economic dogma than on an understanding of how things look from a teacher's perspective.

Most of all, merit pay fails to recognize that there are different kinds of motivation. Doing something because you enjoy it for its own sake is utterly unlike doing something to get money or recognition. In fact, researchers have demonstrated repeatedly that the use of such extrinsic inducements often *reduces* intrinsic motivation. The more that people are rewarded, the more they tend to lose interest in whatever they had to do to get the reward. If bonuses and the like can "motivate" some educators, it's only in an extrinsic sense, and often at the cost of undermining their passion for teaching.

For example, a recent study of a merit pay plan that covered all employees at a northeastern college found that intrinsic motivation declined as a direct result of the plan's adoption, particularly for some of the school's "most valued employees—those who were highly motivated intrinsically before the program was implemented." The more the plan did what it was intended to do—raise people's extrinsic motivation by getting them to see how their performance would affect their salary—the less pleasure they came to take in their work. The plan was abandoned after one year.

That study didn't even take account of how resentful and demoralized people may become when they *don't* get the bonus they're expecting. For all these reasons, I tell Fortune 500 executives (or at least those foolish enough to ask me) that the best formula for compensation is this: Pay people well, pay them fairly, and then do everything possible to help them forget about money. All pay-for-performance plans, of course, violate that last precept.

4. Measurement issues. Despite what is widely assumed by economists and behaviorists, some things are more than the sum of their parts and some things can't be reduced to numbers. It's an illusion to think we can specify and quantify all the components of good teaching and learning, much less establish criteria for receiving a bonus that will eliminate the perception of arbitrariness. No less an authority than the statistician *cum* Quality guru W. Edwards Deming reminded us that "the most important things we need to manage can't be measured."

It may be possible to evaluate the quality of teaching, but it's not possible to reach consensus on a valid and reliable way to pin down the meaning of success, particularly when dollars hang in the balance. What's more, evaluation may eclipse other goals. After merit pay plans take effect, administrators often visit classrooms more to judge teachers than to offer them feedback for the purpose of improvement.

All these concerns apply even when technicians struggle to find *good* criteria for allocating merit pay. But the problems are multiplied when the criteria are dubious, such as raising student test scores. These tests, as I and others have argued elsewhere, tend to measure what matters least. They reflect children's backgrounds more than the quality of a given teacher or school. Moreover, merit pay based on those scores is not only unfair but damaging if it accelerates the exodus of teachers from troubled schools where they're most needed.

Schoolwide merit pay, again, is no less destructive than the individual version. High stakes induce cheating, gaming, teaching to the test, and other ways of snagging the bonus (or dodging the penalty) without actually improving student learning. In fact, some teachers who might resist these temptations, preferring to do what's best for kids rather than for their own wallets, feel compelled to do more test prep when their colleagues' paychecks are affected by the school's overall scores.

It may be vanity or, again, myopia that persuades technicians, even after the umpteenth failure, that merit pay need only be returned to the shop for another tune-up. Perhaps some of the issues mentioned here can be addressed, but most are inherent to the very idea of paying educators on the basis of how close they've come to someone's definition of successful performance. It's time we acknowledged not only that such programs don't work, but that they *can't* work.

Furthermore, efforts to solve one problem often trigger new ones. Late-model merit pay plans often include such lengthy lists of criteria and complex statistical controls that no one except their designers understands how the damn things work.

So how should we reward teachers? We shouldn't. They're not pets. Rather, teachers should be paid well, freed from misguided mandates, treated with respect, and provided with the support they need to help their students become increasingly proficient and enthusiastic learners.

18. Professors Who Profess: Making a Difference as Scholar-Activists

The smart way to keep people passive and obedient is to strictly limit the spectrum of acceptable opinion, but allow very lively debate within that spectrum—even encourage the more critical and dissident views. That gives people the sense that there's free thinking going on, while all the time the presuppositions of the system are being reinforced by the limits put on the range of the debate.

—NOAM CHOMSKY (1998)

It is still disturbingly common to witness what the sociologist Alvin Gouldner (1973, p. 24) once referred to as the "vain ritual of moral neutrality." The assumption that it is possible, or even obligatory, to avoid taking a moral stand in one's work is partly due to the persistent and rather desperate attempt of many social scientists to align themselves with the natural sciences and snub the humanities, which are regarded as soft, subjective, and less substantive. This alliance manifests itself in different ways, ranging from the belief that everything can (and should) be reduced to numbers, to the current fashion for supporting certain pedagogical practices by certifying them as "brain-based." The attempt to bask in the reflected glory of the hard sciences helps to explain why many professors refuse to profess. After all, values are tantamount to biases, something to be excluded or denied. The scientist's job is simply to discover.

But a number of critics over the last century have contended that it is futile, and therefore disingenuous, to pretend that social science can ever be value-free. Some have noted that there are political consequences to that charade: When you take pains to

Originally published in the *Kappa Delta Pi Record* in 2003.

avoid making a value judgment, you end up tacitly accepting the values of the status quo. "Research rooted in the dominant values of the society is less likely to be questioned about its scientific objectivity and yet more likely to suffer from the lack of it," observed Herbert Kelman (1968, p. 72).

Thus, it is seen as perfectly acceptable to ask whether a given educational policy (say, single-sex schooling) succeeds in encouraging more girls to choose careers in fields that have traditionally been dominated by men. But what would we make of a study that asked how successful an intervention has been in encouraging more boys to choose to be nurses, or preschool teachers, or full-time parents? (See Noddings 2002, p. 57.) The latter project is more likely to be dismissed as an attempt to further someone's ideological agenda, but only because the values embedded in the former project are more widely shared.

Other examples aren't hard to find. Some years ago, after I gave a talk about how students can be helped to care about others, a woman rose to inform me, rather heatedly, that she doesn't send her child to school to "learn to be nice." That, she declared, would be "social engineering." But a moment later she added that her child ought to be taught to respect authority. The moral here is that whether one is thought to be engaged in social engineering (or in value-laden research) is determined to a large extent by the particular values in question.

These days many of the talks I give at conferences are about the harmful effects of the Tougher Standards movement, and a number of conference organizers have made a point of "balancing" my presentation by inviting another speaker who supports the conventional wisdom about the need to demand accountability, raise scores, and so on. (Alternatively, I am sometimes asked if I will participate in a debate on the topic so that attendees "can hear both sides.") Yet I am unaware of any organizations that feel the same obligation to provide equal time to the dissident view after inviting a keynote speaker who supports standards and testing. Indeed, mainstream education groups regularly hold entire conferences devoted to the question of how to implement standards-based reform, without a single presenter who inquires whether this is a good idea.

Hidden Values

The same general point can be made by scrutinizing favored concepts in educational research. Consider the idea of *withitness,* the rather cute term coined by Jacob Kounin to denote a teacher who not only is attentive to what students are doing but lets them know she is aware of what's going on. Such teachers were shown to be more effective than their (withoutit?) colleagues. But what does it mean in this context to be "effective"? To Kounin (1970), it meant getting "conformity and obedience"; it meant students didn't do whatever was defined as "deviant" and they kept busy at "the assigned work." Now, if a good classroom is one where students simply do what they're told, it shouldn't be surprising that this is more likely to happen when teachers make it clear they can quickly spot noncompliance. By the same token, if a good society was defined as one where citizens obeyed every governmental decree, then scholars might be able to adduce scientific evidence that the most "effective" leader was one who resembled Orwell's Big Brother.

Come to think of it, "Orwellian" is not a bad description for another common educational construct: *curriculum alignment,* which, at least in its current usage, signifies that what teachers do in the classroom should be made to coincide with something else—usually a test or a list of standards mandated by the state. Those who are reminded of the need for such alignment are actually being exhorted to teach certain material (or teach it in a certain way) not because this enriches students' understanding, or responds to their interests, or is consistent with good research, but simply because someone in power demanded that they do so.

In short, what stands out about many concepts in our field is the way certain values hide behind the appearance of neutral scholarship.

Erroneous Assumptions

If any issue has begun to rouse teacher educators and others in the field to take a public stand, it is the practice of high-stakes testing—of children and of teacher candidates. The current accountability fad was not initiated by educators—either teachers or researchers—nor was it initiated for educational reasons. It was imposed on schools by politicians (and corporate executives) for political reasons. Everything about the way the movement has played out can be traced back to that fact about its birth. The apparent intent of the 1983 "Nation at Risk" report—which David Berliner and Bruce Biddle (1995), among others, have shown to be based on misleading claims and a tendentious use of data—was to cultivate a distrust of public schooling. The current testing mania is a perfectly logical consequence of that perfectly political document.

(Something rather similar, and in a way even more remarkable, took place in Ontario, Canada. In September 1995, John Snobelen, the minister of education and training for Ontario's newly elected Conservative government, announced to his senior staff that their job was to "invent a crisis" in education. To do so, he added, required "some skill" because the schools were actually in better shape than he had thought. His government proceeded to cite that alleged crisis on a regular basis in order to justify a U.S.-style emphasis on standardized testing and accountability. That the crisis was created rather than discovered is a fact known only because a videotape of Snobelen's speech was leaked to the press.)

When I am asked by reporters how we are supposed to hold schools accountable if not by standardized tests, I always pause before describing alternative assessments to explore the premise of the question. We have an obligation, I think, to refuse to accept the debate as it has been framed for us. We need to ask: What is the source of this fierce, frantic demand for accountability? How accurate are the assumptions that underlie it? Who benefits and who loses when this becomes our primary focus?

Are these questions value-laden? Absolutely—as is the question about how we can best hold schools accountable. It's just that the latter inquiry is more common these days, and seemingly more straightforward, so we don't notice the values that inform it.

Against Test Scores as Measures

The next question, then, must be: How can we make a difference? To begin with, we have to acknowledge that conducting and publishing research is not sufficient. Consider the practice of forcing students to repeat a grade: Retention has grown in popularity "during the very time period that research has revealed its negative effects on those retained" (Natriello 1998, p. 15). Nevertheless, there are ways that researchers can maximize their impact on public policy. First, they can make more of an effort to publicize their findings and those of their colleagues, using their credibility as experts to speak up at local gatherings (such as school board meetings), write op-eds for newspapers, meet with legislators and education reporters, and so forth. The people who crusade for "accountability" do not, as a rule, subscribe to the *American Educational Research Journal,* so the findings published there will not have an appreciable impact on policy until they are communicated to other audiences by other means.

(To communicate those findings, of course, requires that we speak and write in a language that is widely understood. Some scholars have slipped so far into the stylized talk—excuse me, discourse—of academia that important ideas are rendered virtually incomprehensible to most people. Because it sometimes seems that scholarship is valued by other academics in direct proportion to its inaccessibility, some individuals may have an instinctive aversion to writing in simple sentences even if they could remember how to do so. The reality is that we contribute usefully to a discussion about testing when we explain clearly why higher scores do not necessarily signal better learning. We do not contribute usefully when we ramble on to a general audience about point-biserial correlations—or, for that matter, about liberatory praxis.)

A constructive effect on real-world policies depends not only on how findings are described but also on how research is conducted in the first place. This comprises not only which topics are selected for investigation, but also how a study is designed and, specifically, what will be the dependent variables. Consider an investigation of the effects of teacher certification. It's understandable that one might be tempted to ask whether certification affects students' scores on standardized tests. Even someone who has his doubts about the value of these tests might reason that many people place stock in those scores and it can be persuasive to show that a given practice has the effect of raising them. But there are long-term consequences to that choice. I believe we should hesitate not only before conducting studies, but even before citing studies, that purport to justify practices we may happen to support—or to indict practices we may oppose—on the basis of their effect on standardized-test results.

I say this for two reasons. First, these tests measure what matters least—or, if you prefer Ralph Tyler's phrase, they give "small answers to small questions." Indeed, such tests are so fundamentally flawed that advocating a given intervention solely because it helps students do better on those tests is not rational. To put it another way, if all one can say in support of a policy or practice (for example, one of those scripted reading programs) is that it has a positive effect on standardized-test results, then one has not yet made a persuasive argument in its behalf. This is particularly true of norm-referenced tests, like the Stanfords, Iowas, or Terra Novas, which were designed to maximize response variance—that is, to create a broad range of scores for the purpose of sorting students efficiently—rather than to gauge whether a given teaching strategy was effective. Such tests are not merely inappropriate as a strategy to *change* teaching (that is, as a high-stakes accountability tool) but also problematic when employed to *measure* teaching. It is not merely a matter of how these tests are used but how they are constructed; some elements of their design raise questions about both applications.

Second, every time a study is published—particularly in a reputable journal or by a reputable researcher—that uses standardized-test scores as the primary dependent variable, those tests gain further legitimacy. If we are not keen on bolstering their reputation and perpetuating their use in schools, we would want to avoid relying on them even in the course of pursuing other objectives and investigating other topics. For example, although I have grave concerns about the extent to which voucher programs help most students (to say nothing about how they undermine public schooling and subsidize religion), I would not try to make this case by citing evidence that these programs fail to raise test scores.

Researchers who understand the dimensions of the threat posed by standardized testing might want to consider (1) using other measures of achievement instead, (2) reinforcing the message that test scores are a poor indicator of student learning by explaining in each study *why* they are not being used, and (3) looking at outcomes other than achievement. Among the possibilities that come to mind here is the construct sometimes known as *continuing motivation to learn.*

This outcome merits attention in itself, not merely in the context of looking for alternatives to test scores. One might go so far as to say that a study in educational psychology is incomplete if it does not consider the impact of its independent variable(s) on how students come to regard what they're doing. Dewey (1916, p.100) famously said that the goal of education is more education: The point is not just to fill students with facts and skills but to nourish their curiosity and disposition to learn. Nor is this view confined to theorists: Many classroom teachers, asked to specify their long-term goals for students, instantly respond with the phrase "lifelong learners."

Forget the test scores. Do smaller classes make kids more likely to enjoy the process of figuring things out? Does a given approach to reading instruction have an effect on whether children pick up books on their own? How do students in bilingual programs feel about school? Even people who regard academic performance as the educational holy grail will have to concede that interest (intrinsic motivation) is a uniquely powerful predictor of achievement. But surely anyone who views interest as an end, not merely a means, ought to be doing research that reflects that conviction.

Teaching Future Educators

Finally, in addition to speaking to the general public about research and reflecting on the design of that research, there is the question of how future teachers are taught. Does that process consist of socializing students to deal with reality as they find it, to accept and perpetuate the status quo, to try to succeed within given parameters? Or are students encouraged to ask radical questions, those that get to the root of the issue? For example, are they more likely to ask how best to raise standardized test scores, or to step back and ask whether such tests need to be used at all?

Why are there Methods courses in schools of education, but no Goals courses? What are our long-term objectives for future educators? Presumably all of us want them to enter the classroom with a set of skills, with knowledge about their subject matter, with a growing competence at (and passion for) teaching itself. But perhaps they also need to develop—or at least avoid losing— a sense of outrage when outrage is required by the situation in which they find themselves. Students may need to hear about different theories of education, but they also need what Hemingway called a crap detector. And perhaps they also ought to acquire a collaborative orientation so that when they are told to hand out worksheets, or run lecture-based and textbook-driven lessons, or spend time giving kids practice tests, their first instinct will be to reach out to their colleagues, to organize, to say, "We must not let this pass." I hope the next generation of teachers emerges from the university secure in the belief that one can and must fight what is wrong, rather than being inclined to put their heads down and hope it will go away by itself. Do schools of education accomplish these goals—and, if not, what can we do to change that state of affairs?

Of course, short of helping students to oppose bad policies, it would be an improvement just to have them work to minimize the damage. In either case, though, they first must understand that these policies are in fact damaging. And that, in turn, requires them to understand that their ultimate obligation is not to raise scores, not to maintain order, not to please administrators, but to do what is best for children. Do preservice programs teach this, emphasize this, every day?

Some of what I am urging may require that teacher educators look at their own teaching. It is not uncommon to find university instructors who see themselves as critical thinkers, progressive and even radical critics of the status quo, but who rely on traditional pedagogical methods to transmit these ideas. Some of their courses are done to, rather than designed with, students—with syllabuses completed before the course has even begun. Some of these instructors proceed largely by lecturing, by fishing for the "right" answers during discussions, even by giving grades. And that is the chief lesson their students will take away: not the explicit content of the course, but the idea that classrooms are places where students listen and memorize facts and figure out how to snag a good mark. (This is precisely parallel to what readers will take away from a study showing that a given intervention produces higher test scores: not merely the explicit finding but the idea that test scores are a reasonable measure of learning.) In both cases, we can do better—provided that we are unafraid of embracing certain values, provided that we are ready to take a stand.

References

Berliner, D. C., and B. J. Biddle. 1995. *The Manufactured Crisis: Myths, Fraud, and the Attack on America's Public Schools.* Reading, Mass.: Addison-Wesley.

Chomsky, N. 1998. *The Common Good.* Interview by D. Barsamian. Tucson, Ariz.: Odonian Press.

Dewey, J. 1916. *Democracy and Education.* New York: Macmillan.

Gouldner, A. W. 1973. "Anti-Minotaur: The Myth of a Value-Free Sociology." In *For Sociology*. New York: Basic.

Kelman, H. C. 1968. *A Time to Speak: On Human Values and Social Research*. San Francisco: Jossey-Bass.

Kounin, J. S. 1970. *Discipline and Group Management in Classrooms*. New York: Holt, Rinehart and Winston.

Natriello, G. 1998. "Failing Grades for Retention." *The School Administrator*, 55, no. 7: 14–17.

Noddings, N. 2002. "The Care Tradition." In *Educating Moral People*. New York: Teachers College Press.

Credits

Chapter 1, What Does It Mean to Be Well Educated?, was originally published in *Principal Leadership,* March 2003, pp. 24–28.

Chapter 2, Turning Learning into a Business, was originally published under the title "The 500-Pound Gorilla," in *Phi Delta Kappan,* October 2002, pp. 113–19. It was adapted from introductory material in *Education, Inc.,* revised edition, edited by Alfie Kohn and Patrick Shannon (Portsmouth, N.H.: Heinemann, 2002).

Chapter 3, The Costs of Overemphasizing Achievement, was originally published in *School Administrator,* November 1999, pp. 40–46.

Chapter 4, Confusing Harder with Better, was originally published in *Education Week,* September 15, 1999, pp. 68, 52.

Chapter 5, Beware of the Standards, Not Just the Tests, was originally published in *Education Week,* September 26, 2001, pp. 52, 38.

Chapter 6, Standardized Testing and Its Victims, was originally published in *Education Week,* September 27, 2000, pp. 60, 46–47.

Chapter 7, Sacrificing Learning for Higher Scores, was originally published under the title "Emphasis on Testing Leads to Sacrifices in Other Areas," in *USA Today,* August 22, 2001, p. 15–A.

Chapter 8, Two Cheers for an End to the SAT, was originally published in the *Chronicle of Higher Education,* March 9, 2001, pp. B12–B13.

Chapter 9, From Degrading to De-Grading, was originally published in *High School Magazine,* March 1999, pp. 38–43.

Chapter 10, The Dangerous Myth of Grade Inflation, was originally published in the *Chronicle of Higher Education,* November 8, 2002, pp. B7–B9.

Chapter 11, Five Reasons to Stop Saying "Good Job!", was originally published in *Young Children,* September 2001, pp. 24–28. An earlier version was published under the title "Hooked on Praise," in *Parents* magazine, May 2000, pp. 39–41.

Chapter 12, Constant Frustration and Occasional Violence, was originally published in *American School Board Journal,* September 1999, pp. 20–24.

Chapter 13, September 11, was originally published under the title "Teaching About Sept. 11," in *Rethinking Schools,* Winter 2001–2002, p. 5.

Chapter 14, A Fresh Look at Abraham Maslow, was originally published under the title "A Look at Maslow's 'Basic Propositions,'" in *Perceiving, Behaving, Becoming: Lessons Learned,* edited by H. Jerome Freiberg (Alexandria, Va.: Association for Supervision and Curriculum Development, 1999).

Chapter 15, Almost There, But Not Quite, was originally published in *Educational Leadership,* March 2003, pp. 26–29.

Chapter 16, Education's Rotten Apples, was originally published in *Education Week,* September 18, 2002, pp. 48, 36–37.

Chapter 17, The Folly of Merit Pay, was originally published in *Education Week,* September 17, 2003, pp. 44, 31.

Chapter 18, Professors Who Profess, was originally published in *Kappa Delta Pi Record,* Spring 2003, pp. 108–113.

Index

accountability
  effects of:
    in conjunction with high-
      quality assessments, 163–65
    on instruction, 42, 120
    on students, 7
    on teachers, 166–67
  and merit pay, 169
  origin of current version of,
    177–78
  and overemphasis on quan-
    tification, 49
  and privatization, 19
  selective application of, 169
  See also standardized testing:
    high-stakes; standards: as
    mandates
Achieve, Inc., 52
achievement
  attribution of, to ability vs.
    effort, 34–36
  effects on:
    of grades, 76–77, 82, 103–105,
      160–61
    of praise, 109
    of stringent grading, 101
  overall trends in, 97, 177
  overemphasis on, 30–37
Adelman, Clifford, 94
advertisements in schools, 13, 26n6
affirmative action, 68
African-American students. *See*
  minority students
Allen, Woody, 5
American Academy of Arts and
  Sciences, 95–96
Amis, Martin, 129–30

assessment, 8–9, 28–37, 49–50,
  76–77, 83–84, 95, 160–61. *See also*
  grades; standardized testing
athletes, glorification of, 126–27n5
Atkinson, Richard C., 65–66, 68, 70

"back to basics" instruction, xi,
  42–43. *See also* education: as
  acquisition of facts
Baker, Mike, 167
Barber, Benjamin, 16
Beane, James, 46
behaviorism, xii–xiii, 49, 109, 137, 170
Benedict, Ruth, 143
Berliner, David, 97, 177
Best Practice High School, 9
Betts, Julian, 101
Biddle, Bruce, 97, 177
Blanco, Maria, 67
Bruner, Jerome, 42
business
  advertising by, in schools, 13
  goals of, for education, 2, 17–18,
    22–23
  influence of, on education, 15,
    19–22, 24–25
  materials by, in school curricula,
    13–14
  ownership of schools by, 14
  pedagogical preferences of,
    23–24
  and standardized testing, 11–12,
    18–19
Business Roundtable, 21, 23, 27n19
Business Task Force on Student
  Standards, 21
Butler, Ruth, 160–61

Central Park East Secondary School, 9
challenge, academic
    avoidance of, by students, 32–33,
        76
    overemphasis on, 44, 101–102
Channel One, 13
cheating, 78, 172
Chomsky, Noam, 174
Chubb, John, 16
class rank. *See* grades: and
    competition
classroom management. *See* disci-
    pline policies
Cohen, David K., 152–53
College Board, 65–68
colleges
    allegations of grade inflation in,
        93–105
    criteria for admission to, 65–71,
        82, 86–88, 123
    overemphasis on admission to,
        85–86, 125
    pedagogy in, 183
    standards movement and, 19
Columbine High School, 117, 124,
    126n5
Committee for Economic Develop-
    ment, 21
competition
    among cooperative groups,
        162
    as deficiency-motivated, 137–38
    emphasis on, by business inter-
        ests, 21, 24
    and grades, 29, 69, 79, 99–101,
        119–20
    among schools and teachers, xi,
        15, 169–70
conflict resolution programs, 162
constructivism, 23, 138

control
    of school policies, 6–7, 51–52, 163–64
    of students, 120, 151–52, 154, 161–62
    of teachers, 169
cooperative learning, 79, 162
Core Knowledge model, 4–6, 7
corporations. *See* business
Creighton, Joanne, 70
Cuban, Larry, 167–68
Cubberley, Ellwood, 20, 21
"cultural literacy," 5
Cureton, Jeanette, 94
curriculum
    "alignment" of, 51, 176–77
    corporate materials used in, 13–14
    relation of, to student behavior,
        155–56
    standards for, 46–53
    student involvement in designing,
        48, 154

Daniels, Harvey, 9
Darling-Hammond, Linda, 20–21,
    118–19, 122
deCharms, Richard, 140
Deci, Edward, 102–3, 136
Deming, W. Edwards, 172
DeVries, Rheta, 106
Dewey, John, 10, 43, 125, 181
De Zouche, Dorothy, 82
difficulty. *See* challenge, academic
direct instruction, 159–60
discipline policies, 123–24, 151–57
Dreikurs, Rudolf, 151
Dweck, Carol, 36

Edison, Inc., 17
education
    as acquisition of facts, 4–6, 43,
        48, 120

based on teaching principles vs.
procedures, 159–60
factory model of, 19, 20, 22, 84
goals and purposes of, xii–xv, 2,
17–18, 22–23, 130, 182–83
judging the quality of an individual's, 1–10
Maslow's views on, 143–45
privatization of, ix–xii, 14–17,
18–19
progressive vs. traditional, 8, 159
research in, 176–81
standardization of, 50
summary of problems with, xi
of teachers, 181–83
top-down control of, 6–7, 51–52,
163–64
as vocational preparation, 4,
17–18
Educational Testing Service (ETS),
12, 122
effort, 34–36
Eisner, Elliot, 46
Eison, James, 100, 104
existentialism, 133

factory model of education, 19, 20,
22, 84
failure, responses to, 33–34
FairTest, 65–66
Finn, Chester E., Jr., 52
French, Marilyn, 28
Fromm, Erich, 132

Gardner, Howard, 48
Geertz, Clifford, 143
generosity, 109, 112
Glasser, William, 136
Goodlad, John, xii
Gouldner, Alvin, 174

grades
alleged inflation of, 81, 93–105
attitudes toward, 75, 78–82,
84–86
and competition, 29, 69, 79,
99–101
as criteria for college admission,
68–69, 82, 86–88
destructive effects of, xiii–xiv,
69, 75–80, 103–105, 160–61
elimination of, in college, 104
elimination of, in high school,
80–85, 88–90, 123
lack of predictive value of, 70,
100
minimizing harms of, 85–86
purposes of, 28–29
vs. other forms of assessment,
76–77, 83–84
See also achievement: overemphasis on; assessment
Grogger, Jeff, 101
Grusec, Joan, 109

habits of mind, 9
Harcourt Educational Measurement,
12
Harlow, Harry, 140
Harvard University
claims of grade inflation at, 93,
96, 99
preparation for admission to,
85–86
health, psychological, 131–36, 145
higher education. See colleges
"higher expectations," 58–59
high school
education in, 8–9, 120
grades in, 75–90
problems with, 118–21

reform of, 122–23
shootings in, 117–18, 120–21, 124–25
standardized testing in, 6–7, 55–56
high-stakes tests. *See* standardized testing: high-stakes
Holt, Maurice, 169
homeschooling, 87
Houghton Mifflin, 17
Howe, Harold II, 48
human nature, 132–33, 135–36, 143

incentives. *See* merit pay; motivation: intrinsic vs. extrinsic
individualism, 142–43
intelligence, 34–36
interest in learning
  as dependent variable, 181
  effect on:
    of grades, 75–76, 102–104, 160–61
    of overemphasis on achievement, 31
    of praise, 109
  as goal of education, 9–10, 181
  See also motivation, intrinsic vs. extrinsic

Jahoda, Marie, 132
Jones, Ken, 164

Katz, Lilian, 108
Kelman, Herbert, 175
Kentucky Education Reform Act, 164–65
Koestner, Richard, 102–3
Kohlberg, Lawrence, 146*n*
Kounin, Jacob, 176
Kozol, Jonathan, 11
Kunc, Norman, 153

Labaree, David, 16
Learning First Alliance, 46
Levine, Arthur, 94
Levine, Eliot, 9
low-income students, testing of, 56–61

Maehr, Martin, 37
Mansfield, Harvey, 93, 99, 100
market values, 22–23. *See also* privatization
Marriott, Donna, 153–54
Maryland State Performance Assessment Program, 164–65
Maslow, Abraham
  and education, 143–45
  health as defined by, 133–36
  health as focus of, 131–32, 136, 145
  individualism of, 142–43
  personal characteristics of, 131
  and self-actualization, 131, 137–39, 142
  and theory of needs and motivation, 136–43
  and view of human nature, 132–33, 135–36
May, Rollo, 133
McClelland, David, 69–70
McGraw-Hill, 11–12
McNeil, Linda, 49, 62, 121
measurement, 49–50, 171–72
Meier, Deborah, 9, 16–17, 45, 46, 61, 118, 125
merit pay, 167–73
Met School, 9
Midgley, Carol, 37
Milton, Ohmer, 100, 104
minority students
  admission of, to college, 67–68
  testing of, 56–61

misbehavior, responses to, 111, 153–57
motivation
    intrinsic vs. extrinsic, 32, 102–103, 108–109, 139–40, 163, 170–71
    Maslow's theory of, 136–43
    of teachers, 166–67, 170–71
    See also interest in learning

National Assessment of Educational Progress (NAEP), 97
National Association of Manufacturers, 21
"Nation at Risk" report, 97, 177
naturalistic fallacy, 134–36
NCS Pearson, 12
needs
    Maslow's theory of, 136–43
    of students in high school, 118–21
    vs. obedience as schools' focus, 124, 136, 152
Nelson, Wade, 168
Nicholls, John, 151
Noddings, Nel, 2, 46, 175

Ohanian, Susan, 46
Ontario, Canada, 177–78

parents
    focus on college admission by, 125
    support for grades by, 84–85
    support for traditional education by, 122–23
pay for performance. *See* merit pay
Perry, Michelle, 159–60, 161
"political correctness," 98
Pollio, Howard, 100, 104

Popham, W. James, 29, 57
Powell, Brian, 66
praise
    alternatives to, 111–13
    pervasiveness of, 106, 156
    undesirable effects of, 106–110, 156–57
privatization, ix–xii, 14–17, 18–19
progressive education, 8, 159
public education, attacks on. *See* privatization
punishment, 106, 124, 161–62

Quality Counts, 46
quantification, 49–50, 171–72

reading incentives, 162–63
report cards. *See* grades
research, educational, 176–81
retention, 178
rewards. *See* motivation: intrinsic vs. extrinsic; praise; reading incentives
Riverside Publishing, 12, 17
Rogers, Carl, 132
Rosovsky, Henry, 96
Rowe, Mary Budd, 107
Ryan, Richard, 102–3, 136

SAT, 65–68, 96–97
school choice plans. *See* privatization
schooling. *See* education
"school reform," meaning of, ix–xii
school-to-work programs, 17
seat time, 4
self-actualization, 131, 137–39, 142
self-discipline, 156

September 11 attacks, 128–30
Sinclair, Upton, 144
Sizer, Ted, 9, 121
Snobelen, John, 177–78
socioeconomic status, 54, 66. *See also* low-income students, testing of
Spring, Joel, 25
Standard & Poors, 11
standardized testing
    as basis for merit pay, 172
    benefits of, to business, 12, 18–19
    effects of:
        on educators, 56, 60, 166–67
        on low-income and minority students, 56–61
        on teaching and learning, 56, 58–59, 62–64
    extent of, 54
    high-stakes, 6–7, 55–56, 59–61, 164–65, 172, 177
    inappropriateness of, to assess learning, 4, 29, 54–55, 66–67
    norm-referenced, 29, 54–55, 57, 180
    opposition to, 46, 178
    overall trend in results of, 97
    and privatization, ix–x, 18–19
    relation of, to standards, 46–47, 53
    use of, in research, 179–81
    of young children, 55
    See also SAT; standards
standards
    absence of criticism of, 46, 53
    grade-by-grade, 50–51
    as mandates, 7, 30, 51–52
    meaningful, 9
    outcome vs. content, 47

outcome vs. opportunity, 59–60
    quantifiability of, 49–50
    ratings of states', 52–53
    relation of, to tests, 46–47, 53
    specificity of, 47–48
    tougher or higher, 41–45, 61, 101–102, 120
    uniformity of, 50–51
Steelman, Lala Carr, 66
Stotsky, Sandra, 49–50
Strickland, Dorothy, 58
Success for All, 63
systemic perspective, 154–55, 170

teachers
    compensation of, 166–73
    competition among, 169–70
    control of, 169
    discipline policies of, 151–57
    education of, 181–83
    effects on, of standardized testing, 56, 60, 166–67
    motivation of, 166–67, 170–71
tests. *See* standardized testing
Thoreau, Henry David, 45
traditional education. *See* "back to basics" instruction; education: progressive vs. traditional
Tyack, David, 167–68
Tyler, Ralph, 179

universities. *See* colleges

Valenzuela, Angela, 62
values
    in educational policies, 175–76
    in educational research, 176–77
    in social science, 174–75

violence
     and schools, 117–18, 120–21,
          124–25, 126n1
     and U.S. foreign policy,
          128–29
vouchers. *See* privatization

Wellstone, Paul, 57
White, Robert, 140
Whitehead, Alfred North, 4
Whitford, Betty Lou, 164
workers, students viewed as, 17

zero-tolerance policies, 124